Is the Apple Really Red?

Is the Apple Really Red?

10 Essays on Science and Religion

Ashish Dalela

SHABDA
PRESS

Is the Apple Really Red?—10 Essays on Religion and Science
by Ashish Dalela
www.shabda.co

Published by Shabda Press
www.press.shabda.co
ISBN 978-81930523-5-8
v1.5(05/2021)

Dedicated to His Divine Grace A.C. Bhaktivedanta Swami Prabhupāda, who saw the development of a true understanding of material nature as an essential part of the advancement in religion.

Contents

Preface

I have been studying Vedic philosophy and exploring its connection to modern science since 1993. In 2008, after nearly 15 years of this study, I wrote a book entitled *Vedic Creationism* in which I discussed some of the ideas that connect theories of matter in modern science, their current unsolved problems, and how these problems could be addressed by adopting a different approach to the study of matter. I called this approach a *semantic* theory of nature. Vedic Creationism was a large effort and it took me two years to complete. At the end of writing it, I had the outline of an approach that could be used to evolve science, solve its currently unsolved problems, while demonstrating the relevance of Vedic theories to the study of matter.

As I interacted with the readers of *Vedic Creationism*, I realized that the book was too encompassing and dense, especially for someone unfamiliar with Vedic ideas. It tried to bite more than it could completely chew, while leaving out several arguments which were necessary for a more convincing connection between Vedic philosophy and modern science. Then, I began the effort of dividing the ideas in *Vedic Creationism* into smaller, more digestible chunks.

I also realized that many people would be put off by the notion that a book discussing advances in science also talks about religion, when, in fact, most problems in science and their possible solutions can be discussed without reference to scripture. For this audience, it was necessary to frame a different set of arguments based on reason and experience, although arriving at the same conclusion—a practice that prevailed in ancient India but died over the centuries.

Attempts to present the ideas in *Vedic Creationism* in a more digestible, accessible, and relevant format have so far resulted in four books: (1) *Six Causes: The Vedic Theory of Creation*, (2) *Sāṅkhya and Science: Applications of Vedic Philosophy to Modern Science*, (3) *Quantum*

Meaning: A Semantic Interpretation of Quantum Theory, and (4) *Gödel's Mistake: The Role of Meaning in Mathematics*. The first two are focused on Vedic philosophy while the last two discuss scientific problems and their solutions without reference to Vedic ideas. Together, these books present the same argument that I originally wrote in *Vedic Creationism*, but in much smaller and more focused topics. The arguments are considerably more elaborated and organized logically, without some of the liberties that I took earlier.

I was now faced with a different problem, namely that of providing a concise introduction to these different books so that readers could quickly understand the big picture before they delve into the nitty-gritty details on which the big picture rests. This particular book hopes to provide that gentle introduction to the same ideas that are described in greater detail in the other books.

The crux of the problem this book tries to address is the conflict between religion and science. Science formulates theories of matter, while religion deals in questions of the soul, God, afterlife, and morality. Today, these two are on a collision course. Many religious people seek rational justifications for their faith, but the reasons they think actually justify God or the soul are often not very convincing. Many scientists similarly seek a better understanding of the mind and consciousness from within science but that search is often thwarted by the concepts about matter, space, and time in current science. Over the course of years of my study, it has become increasingly clear to me that the reconciliation of religion and science requires a different approach to both science and religion. Specifically, science needs to develop a theory of matter compatible with the existence of mind and consciousness, and religions need to find a conception of God that can be related to the nature of space, time, and matter.

Vedic philosophy is a conducive starting point in this endeavor because it deals with the theory of how God creates space and time by expanding His experience, and how matter encodes meanings. However, this description of space, time, and matter is radically different than the theories about nature in modern science. While objects are the primary material entity in modern science, meanings are the primary material entity in Vedic philosophy. The shift from a theory of independent objects to a theory of contextual meanings represents a formidable but very fruitful evolution of current science, as I will show. It is formidable because it has the potential to overturn many current assumptions in science. It is fruitful because this change would address many unsolved problems in science.

The books mentioned above and the present one tries to describe the changes that need to be made, their implications for science, and what those changes would entail for our understanding of religion once this exercise about matter has been completed.

The journey from the problems in science, to the idea that the solution of these problems requires a central role for meaning, to the nature of the mind and consciousness that produce these meanings, to an understanding of different types of consciousness, is a rather long one. It has also been made difficult by over four centuries of materialistic thinking devoid of meaning and mind. It is therefore very difficult to paint the whole picture of the necessary changes in a single book that would also carry all the details. This book tries to paint the whole picture, pointing to other books for the details. This approach is particularly relevant for the lay reader. Even astute readers can get an understanding of the map before they undertake the journey and see the territory for themselves. The book does not presuppose any formal understanding of scientific theories, or Vedic philosophy, not even a belief in any other religious ideology. It only assumes that the reader can keep an open mind to new ideas.

The book is divided into ten small essays that discuss common topics of debate and controversy in modern times. Each essay tries to summarize the nature of the debate, the problems that remain outstanding, and what the Vedic view brings to the table. This approach, I think, can help the reader better grasp the reasons for the Vedic view and retain the ideas that will hopefully serve as an easy primer to further more involved and deeper studies in the future.

Since these descriptions are based on Vedic philosophy, it is imperative to clarify and fix many of the misconceptions about it that exist in the modern mind. For instance, many people believe that Vedic theory is fatalistic because it talks about *karma*. Others think that Vedic philosophy is a hodge-podge of impersonalism and polytheism. Finally, very few people know that the Vedic texts also contain a detailed theory of matter. Some essays in this book are intended to clarify these issues and lay the apparent controversies to rest.

While the conventional wisdom about religion is that its notions about the soul, God, morality, and afterlife can never be made scientific, I will argue that these notions can be understood rationally, and would emerge out of a new science based on the study of meanings in matter rather than the description of independent objects. Most theistic scientists and most scientific theists today claim only that science and religion are mutually compatible but not identical. They believe that ideas of soul, God, morality, and afterlife cannot be directly inferred from modern science—they can only be supposed to exist because science itself will not explain them. Atheistic scientists on the other hand claim that the theories of matter are themselves complete without soul, God, morality, and afterlife. Thus, we have the following dilemma at hand: if science is complete then there is no room for God and the soul; if however, science is incomplete then we can believe in God and the soul but we cannot rationally justify their existence based on what can be observed or reasoned.

What you are about to read will, I believe, shake these notions about religion and science. I will argue that science can be complete, and notions about God, soul, afterlife, and morality will be necessitated due to developments in science when science solves its current problems of incompleteness. The completeness of science and the existence of God are therefore not contradictory ideas. Rather, when science has solved the current outstanding problems, it will indicate the existence of God and the soul. This kind of assertion, I believe, has never been made, not even by the most ardently religious people. The premise of the book is quite stunning and, hopefully, by the time you finish reading it, you will see why I make that claim.

1

Is the Apple Really Red?

The Problem of Realism

In the everyday world, when we look at a red apple, we think that the apple is indeed *red*. This idea is called *naïve realism* in Western philosophy and the naiveté pertains to the fact that we attribute sensations back to the objects being perceived. Philosophers in the early days of scientific empiricism argued against naïve realism because, if the world was just the way we perceived it, there would be no perceptual mistakes and hallucinations. Given that there are mistakes and hallucinations, it was natural to suppose a difference between our perception and reality. This difference was attributed to the divide between mind and matter. The mind, it was said, perceives the world in terms of qualities such as color, taste, and smell, while matter does not have these properties. The correct way to describe the objective world, it was now supposed, was to measure objects against other objects rather than against the observer's senses. This led to modern science where reality is described in terms of properties measured against standard objects such as a standard meter, a standard clock, a standard kilogram, etc.

While this approach to science has been quite successful, it is only because the hard problem of understanding why the world of objective properties is perceived as qualities was pushed into the mind. Note that if science must be empirical, then it must use the senses which perceive qualities and not quantities. Therefore, qualities don't disappear from science as far as experiments are concerned. They are only evicted from scientific *theories*. This eviction appears to work in the description of matter independent of the mind but creates issues

1

in studying the mind when the mind is reduced to the brain. If physical objects do not have qualities, and the brain is a physical object, then how can qualities arise in the brain when they do not exist prior in the objects? If, on the other hand, qualities exist in the brain (as perception), then they could also potentially exist in other material objects; this would imply that we can study and describe material objects in terms of qualities as well.

Both these approaches to the brain lead to problems. If a physical theory cannot explain qualities in the brain, then the theory is incomplete because qualities in perception are obviously phenomena to be explained and the physical theory tries and fails to reduce these phenomena to the brain. If, however, the physical theory explains the qualities, then the original eviction of qualities from science was itself wrong: it might now be correct to assume that since the brain has qualities and the brain is material, the world it represents must also have the same qualities since it is also as equally material as the brain.

Mind-Body Dualism

The problem of perception was 'solved' in the philosophy of science by assuming a difference between the mind and the body. Philosophers supposed that the world is not what appears to be because the mind by which the world is perceived is different from matter. This separation has now come back to haunt us when science turns its attention to the mind. Aside from the fact that the mind understands concepts, performs judgments, has intentional relations, and comprehends morals, we also believe that these concepts, judgments, intentions, and morals have an influence on the world of objects. If qualities and quantities are fundamentally different, then how can the world of qualities influence the world of quantities and vice versa? The standard neuroscientific answer to this problem is that the brain is still chemicals and their reactions. For instance, happiness can be characterized by the presence of serotonin. But this still does not solve the problem of the *linguistic* divide between serotonin and happiness. Being serotonin is different from being happy. Should we say that serotonin in the test tube also makes the test tube happy? If not, when does serotonin become happiness? The discovery of chemicals does not solve the problem of perception. Rather, it leads to a different problem: If the mind is different from the body to begin with, then how can the mind be reduced to the body? Conversely, if the mind is actually the body, then why would we describe the body any differently than the qualities in the mind?

The latter position entails that all physical properties in current science must be replaced by perceptual properties. For instance, material objects must be described not in terms of length, mass, energy, momentum, temperature, etc., but rather in terms of color, taste, smell, sound, and touch. When the mind is reduced to the body, either the physical properties must explain the perceptions or the physical properties must be replaced by perceptual qualities. Science is unable to find any mechanism by which the former can be achieved. And trying to attempt the latter entails a fresh beginning in science, discarding all established theories of nature. Would we now prefer to dissolve the mind-body divide or rather live with the divide between the two?

Mind-body dualism is obviously not desirable as it leads to problems in understanding the nature of literature, art, music, and science itself. This is because all these areas of human activity involve meanings. What is meaning? It seems to be a concept attached to physical things. However, if concepts cannot natively exist in material objects—and literature, art music, and scientific theories are material objects—their meanings must also be outside matter. We now have a paradox. Science is about the nature of matter, but the understanding of science is outside matter. In a similar way, something is not a work of art or a piece of music or literature unless there are minds who can understand its meaning. In fact, we could also claim that there is nothing called art, literature, or music. It is *we* who make them art, literature, or music.

Enter post-modernism, which now extends this idea to science itself! Now, there is nothing called a *real* scientific theory. All theories are symbolic descriptions of nature and the meanings of these symbols—i.e. that some symbol denotes some physical property—are our creation. Nature only presents itself as some phenomenon, but we force this phenomenon to fit into some ordered universal concept and theory of nature. Clearly, this force-fitting of phenomena must discard the meanings in the world, because no two individuals agree upon the meanings of the phenomena. They can only be fit into a single theory if their differences were discarded. This discarding of meanings, therefore, represents a particular kind of interpretation of nature, which does not fit everyone's interpretation and does not explain their experiences.

The truth of a scientific theory is thus relative to the community of scientists who selectively discard certain parts of our experiences—namely those that deal in meanings. With a selective appreciation of nature, we create a constrained view of nature which now becomes our scientific theory. It is we who make something into a scientific theory. Science only deals with matter but its meanings have to be understood by some mind. Our lives would be meaningless without literature, art, music, science, and without meanings in general. And science cannot explain meanings, because—as I showed—they were already evicted from matter. Mind-body dualism is therefore not desirable because if the mind is indeed separate from the body, and science is ultimately in the mind, then science must only be an 'interpretation' of the world. As an interpretation, it is no better or worse than another interpretation.

To solve the problem of perception, science created a divide between matter and the mind. This divide leads to problems in the study of the mind. But it also creates problems in understanding the meanings of material objects. If everything is meaningless and we give it meanings, then we cannot attribute those meanings back to the world.

Science is one such meaningful description of nature. However, since we cannot attribute the redness of the apple back to the world, we also cannot attribute scientific concepts and theories back to the world. If the world is not apples and redness then it is also not electrons! After all, both apples and electrons are our concepts. The method by which we know if something is an electron or an apple is observation. If observations are not good enough to tell us if something is an apple, then they are also not adequate to confirm that something is indeed an electron. We must either acknowledge that both electron and apple are mental constructs (and could not be real), or accept that they are both potentially equally real. Scientific theories—the dualist can argue—are not about reality because they deal in concepts such as particles and waves, position and momentum, etc., and all these concepts are always in our minds. How can some concepts be applied to reality and not others?

Some philosophers of science argue that we are allowed to treat scientific ideas as real because they seem to *work*. We can use scientific theories to make predictions about nature. But who can deny that everyday concepts like redness and apple also work? Our lives are filled with the use of everyday concepts—even nebulous ones like liberty, justice, and morality—upon which the everyday world is organized. Using these concepts we are able to navigate an enormously complex world, so these everyday concepts also appear to work in a pragmatic sense. How can the concept of an electron be real but redness not be?

Sensing various difficulties in justifying the reality of any concept, a school of philosophy in the early 20th century—called positivism—argued that there is actually no reality and no concepts either. There are only sensations and words. Each word is tied to some sensation which we call its *meaning*. The meaning of a word is not some mental idea, but in the *things* it refers to. But, if that were so, then how could we *imagine* things that we have never seen? How could we create theories—including those in modern science that are highly counterintuitive? We have never seen curved space-time, electrons, protons, or the Big Bang. How can we speak about them if words are mapped to the things we have seen? Science cannot be done without concepts and conjectures. If nature is matter but not ideas, then it cannot produce science.

Also, if we go down the path of reducing all concepts to sensations, then how can different types of sensations be called out by the same concept? For instance, we can look at different types of objects and call them 'tables.' If there were only sensations, then there could never be tables because all tables will look different in some way. Now we could call language itself an illusion, but that would mean that all science, formulated in mathematics is also an illusion. Mathematics after all depends on concepts such as set, point, and number which cannot be reduced to sensations (this is a deeper point about the nature of mathematical concepts where attempts to reduce them to sensations have been made and they lead to paradoxes; the reader is referred to my book *Gödel's Mistake* for a detailed discussion of these paradoxes).

While the above discussion of the mind-body problem and its various consequences is not exhaustive, hopefully, it gives you a glimpse of what is at stake. Once you accept the mind-body divide, then nothing is sacrosanct. You cannot know reality because that knowledge is concepts, and concepts are not real. You cannot speak, because speech involves concepts and they are not real. You cannot believe anything, because you see qualities, but reality is not any of those qualities. This hopefully convinces you that there is a problem that needs to be solved. The problem has many variations, but it can be reduced to a simple question that I briefly alluded to earlier: *Is the apple really red?* If you say "no" then you have the mind-body problem and its consequences. If you say "yes" then you need a new explanation of the material world: matter would now be explained using perceptual concepts rather than physical concepts. For instance, now, apples will be red, round, and sweet, music and art will be beautiful, and politicians obnoxious.

This new kind of explanation is clearly very hard to approach in modern science, given that all scientific thinking so far has been done by separating the mind from matter. How can we think about matter in a new way, quite different from how it has been thought of so far?

The Vedic View of Realism

In Vedic philosophy, there is a red apple but it is not red in the way we *sense* it. To understand this viewpoint, consider the relation between words and meanings. The word 'red' is also red but not in the sense of the color of redness. The word 'red' represents the *idea* of red as a physical vibration and the meaning of 'red' is the sensation or concept of redness. In the same way, the Vedas state that the external world is 'sound vibrations' which denote the meanings that we can apprehend. These sounds are produced by objectifying—that is, turning into objects—the meanings in the mind. And they are perceived as sensations by converting the sounds into meanings. The external world is, therefore, 'red' as *vāk* or sound (*vāk* literally means speech) while the internal world is red as *manas* or meaning in the mind. *Manas* and *vāk* are connected by *prāṇa* which converts meanings into sounds and sounds into meanings. *Prāṇa* is said to exist within the nervous system in the body which carries signals from the physical world and converts them into ideas in the mind. Similarly, *prāṇa* converts mental ideas into material objects. There is hence a material world that is objective, but these objects are not meaningless. Rather, all objects are symbols of meanings because they originate as ideas, and are objectified into things by the *prāṇa*.

Prāṇa is also the agency that causes us to breathe, and a host of other neurological and biological functions. Vedic philosophy describes that when you speak, *prāṇa* is used to convert the mental idea into speech. Similarly, when you hear or perceive, the *prāṇa* in the sense organs carries the information into the mind whereupon it is perceived as a sensation. The idea that *prāṇa* connects mind and body is widely used as the basis of yoga and meditation, and when a person dies, the *prāṇa* is said to leave the body and detach the mind from that body.

To understand these ideas in a scientific context, we can think of the external world as vibrations, as modern science already does. For instance, in atomic theory, nature is treated as quantized waves. However, unlike science, where these waves are studied as phase, amplitude, and frequency, Vedic philosophy treats them as *phonemes* that represent meanings. These phonemes denote objective *information* but the information is semantic (rather than physical) in the specific sense that it denotes *types* rather than *quantities*. For instance, there can be a sound vibration that denotes the idea of *redness*. This sound encodes the meaning 'red' and therefore the material reality is red. But it is not the sensation of red or the qualitative perception of redness.

Therefore, if you believe that the apple is red, you are right, because the apple is the objective encoding of information about redness. But that does not mean that the apple exists exactly as we perceive it sensually. The apple's redness is the *information* about redness that exists as a sound vibration similar to the word 'red.' The senses gather this information about redness and convert it into the sensation of redness. Reality and perception are therefore both red, but they exist as two different kinds of red—the word 'red' and the meaning 'red.' The body and the mind are therefore mutually connected as words and meanings.

This approach to the description of nature alters the understanding of the mind-body problem because it changes the nature of the body.

The body is now a symbol of the mind: it objectifies the ideas that exist in the mind. Through such objectification, the mind becomes *communicable*. The mind and the body are not to be described using two different languages—qualities and quantities—because matter can be a representation of ideas. Matter and mind can be described by the same *words* although these words denote different things in the case of the mind and the body. In the mind, the word is the perception of an idea, and in the body the word is the objectification of that idea as a symbol.

We would now not describe the world as phase, amplitude, and frequency. We would instead describe it as *phonemes*. What is the difference between a phoneme and phase, amplitude and frequency? The difference is that a phoneme is a type while phase, amplitude, and frequency are quantities. Just as you can write the letter 'A' in different fonts, in different sizes, and in different colors, in the same way, you can also express the phoneme using many different physical vibrations but they will still be the same phoneme. Likewise, the small letter 'l,' the capital letter 'I' and the numeral '1' all look similar, but they are three different types. The difference of types denoted by these symbols entails that physical similarity is not semantic similarity. Indeed, in different contexts, the symbol 'I' could denote the English word representing the self or the first numeral in the sequence of natural numbers.

The meaning in the symbol is sometimes due to its form, and this is when we say that the sound represents meaning. The meaning may also be obtained by the relation between symbols, which is when it becomes contextual. However, to even derive contextual meanings, there must already be some meaning in the object natively. For instance, you can call a block of wood as a 'chair', and the chairness is contextual meaning. But even prior to this contextual meaning there was a possessed meaning which we called a 'block of wood'. So, contextual and possessed meanings are different and complementary, but contextual meaning requires some possessed meaning, though not vice versa. Again, we can use language as an example. To a very large extent, the meaning of sentences has possessed meaning, although sometimes the same sentence can produce an alternative interpretation. If that interpretation wasn't given, the sentence still has a native meaning.

Now when we start speaking about meanings, we quickly realize that we are attributing them to macroscopic objects such as tables and chairs. In classical physics, which described the world as point particles that had no form, we could claim that matter has no form, and hence no meaning. But macroscopic objects obviously have forms. And these forms—e.g. the shape of something—are associated with meanings, such as tables and chairs. This fact leads to new problems in science. The problem is that the collection of particles has additional properties which cannot be understood in terms of the properties of the individual particle. It is thus sometimes colloquially said that the whole is not reducible to parts, because the reduction leads to a loss of meanings.

Present science studies the properties of individual objects, which results in problems of incompleteness when science has to deal with object collections. These problems can be resolved if matter was described as symbols of meanings, rather than physical things. For instance, problems in understanding atomic theory can be understood if the collection is seen as representing meanings rather than just physical properties. This problem is dealt with at length in my book *Quantum Meaning* which interprets the incompleteness of quantum theory as arising out of the fact that matter is not just physical properties but also a symbol of meaning. In other words, meanings are not just interpretations of the physical world created by the mind; meanings also have an objective existence outside the mind. However, we must be musically savvy, artistically inclined, and linguistically literate to read the meaning. This literacy already exists in our senses which can read the objective meaning in matter and transform it into sensations, because there is a natural language in which meanings are encoded and decoded. We can also invent symbolic languages, beyond the natural language.

A new view of matter is needed to explain the world as symbols of meaning rather than merely the physical properties of the symbols. The physical view—which postulates independent objects—works in some cases approximately but fails in atomic theory where the particles are mutually entangled as if they weren't independent anymore but rather parts of a whole. Reductionism fails in atomic theory and we claim that the world is no longer *separable*. This separability has been the cornerstone of classical physics, and it makes atomic theory problematic. The resurrection out of this problem is to say that both atomic particles as well as macroscopic objects are symbols of meaning. The macroscopic world is therefore not classical; it is rather the whole which must be treated semantically, just the parts must be seen semantically. The classical physical view of nature in which matter is only physical properties fails to account for the entanglement of object collections.

A Linguistic Theory of Nature

The Vedic viewpoint presents a type of linguistic realism in which reality is the 'text' which is being processed by the observer. Reality can also be modified by adding 'text' to it similar to how a programmer programs a computer by inputting a computer program into it.

This view of reality forms the basis of the chanting of *mantras* which are sound utterances. The *mantra* is not mumbo-jumbo. Its effects are rather based on the idea that matter is vibrations that represent meaning and can be described as *types* rather than as physical properties. The sound in the *mantra*, therefore, acts on the material reality not as physical properties but as meanings. The magical causal effects of *mantras* can only be explained when we postulate that the frequency and amplitude are not the cause of change. Rather, the cause is the meaning encoded by these vibrations. This type of causality can be understood when nature is perceived as types. There are many ramifications of linguistic realism and they are discussed in my other books, *Sāṅkhya and Science* and *Six Causes*. The application of these ideas to atomic theory, as already mentioned, is discussed in the book *Quantum Meaning*. The problems of meaning and how meanings are encoded through symbols also appear in mathematics and computing theory. These applications are discussed at length in *Gödel's Mistake.*

The idea therefore that matter encodes meanings has many important implications for modern science, specifically in relation to currently unsolved problems. The Vedic view of reality is hence not just a religious viewpoint of the ancient Indians. It is also a viewpoint that is relevant to modern problems in philosophy, mathematics, linguistics, computing, and physics. The Vedic viewpoint tells us that the study of matter in terms of physical properties—e.g., the frequency, amplitude, and wavelength of a sound—is incomplete because that study does not adequately capture the meanings represented by the sound. If meanings have causal properties, then the science of physical properties is incomplete. To the extent that meanings have physical embodiments, this science will describe the world correctly to some extent. But it must ultimately fail because meanings are not identical to physical facts.

A different view of matter is essential before the mind in the observer and the nature of God besides other aspects of religion can be understood. When this view on matter is understood, other mystical and spiritual aspects of Vedic philosophy are also grasped. This view has theoretical and empirical ramifications, which can be used to develop a new kind of science based on meanings. This science will not suffer from the problems of the mind-body dualism mentioned earlier because mind and body will be described using the same *language*. The mind will now perceive the sensation or concept red because the world is a symbol of redness. As this view of the mind is extended, more properties in the mind—such as judgments, intentions, and morals—will also have counterparts in science. This approach is therefore scientifically very fruitful because it identifies new properties in matter that cannot be seen from the current physical viewpoint about nature. These properties can in turn lead to new theories and experiments.

Science and Empiricism

The differences between science and religion are obviously manifest at the level of God, the soul, the afterlife, and morality. But these differences begin in the idea that we have senses and a mind which perceive the world differently than how science describes it today. If I cannot say that the world is red when I perceive redness, then I obviously cannot say that there is a God when I perceive God. To the extent that the perception of redness is an illusion, the perception of God must also be an illusion, because all perceptions—in current science—are illusions as they cannot be applied back to reality. The problem can only be solved if we begin our science by applying our perceptions back to reality. The application begins in sensory perceptions and grows through deeper aspects of the observer such as mind, intelligence, ego, and morality, culminating in the understanding of the soul and God as sources and consumers of meaning. As we delve deeper into the recesses of the observer, we find newer properties that can be applied back to matter.

This application does not reduce mind to matter although it shows that matter can be studied in terms of the properties of the observer. Everything that the observer can potentially perceive can also potentially be real. We, therefore, study matter by finding all the various ways in which we can *experience* it. This is a radical notion of matter, which implies that all experiences are potentially real, and we can find all the material properties by understanding all the experiences. This approach to science begins in experience and not in material objects.

Our experiences do not end with sensations. We also experience concepts, judgments, intentions, and morals. These correspond to the aspects of the observer called mind, intelligence, ego, and the moral sense in Vedic philosophy. These deeper aspects of the observer cannot be reduced to sensations. For instance, a shade of yellow does not preempt the concept of yellow; while the senses perceive the shade of yellow, the mind perceives the concept. If these perceptions are real, then there is a real property in nature that embodies the idea of yellowness beyond the specific shades of yellow. Similarly, there must be real properties in matter that correspond to our experiences of intelligence, ego, and the moral sense. Current science claims that material particles are real and perceptions by the senses, mind, intelligence, and ego are illusions created from that reality. The Vedic view instead says that all perceptions can potentially be real, and our senses of perception can also provide us with the knowledge of the true nature of reality.

If we claim that all experience is an illusion, we must explain the qualities in experience in terms of the physical property quantities in current science, and that project is hopelessly flawed and impossible. If instead we claim that all experience can potentially be real, then we can explain these experiences based on a theory of matter that postulates new properties. If this theory makes new predictions, then it must be real, using the same criterion that makes current theories of science real. The attempt to use the observer's experience as the basis of doing science, therefore, widens the scope of science. It does not change our reliance on reason and experience. Rather, it appeals to deeper forms of reason and experience that are not used in current science.

2

Is Free Will an Illusion?

Libet's Experiments on Free Will

Benjamin Libet's experiments in neuroscience are probably the most debated piece of research exploration in this nearly 40-year-old field of study. The controversial piece of Libet's work is where he shows that neurological activity precedes the conscious reporting of a free will decision by a subject. Libet's work has been used by materialists to argue that free will is an illusion—an afterthought we apply to brain activity. In actuality, the materialists claim, all actions are determined by physical laws outside our control, although we tend to give them volitional interpretation. Do we or do we not have free will? With Libet's experiments, it appears that our first-person experience of volition is illusory. This is a very radical claim in which a third-person report contradicts a first-person report, which is then extended to claim that we are having the illusion of free will.

The basic setup for Libet's experiment is quite simple. A subject, whose brain is wired to MRI equipment, is asked to make decisions—for example, to press a "left" button instead of a "right" one. The subject is asked to report the exact point at which s/he makes a decision, while the experimenter monitors the neurological activity. After the experiment, the subject's reports are correlated with corresponding observed neurological events. The belief in mind-body dualism seems to imply that if the mind controls the body, then conscious choices should come before the observed neurological event. But Libet found the reverse. He showed that the brain activity preceded the conscious reporting by almost 200 milliseconds.

Recently, this experiment was confirmed by John-Dylan Haynes of the Max Planck Institute. Haynes' experiment shows that the brain

14

activity precedes the conscious decision by a full 10 seconds! Of course, there are some differences in the brain areas that Libet and Haynes study. Libet focused on the cortex while Haynes observed the frontopolar and parietal cortex. Nevertheless, the essential conclusion from these findings is the same in both cases: Brain activity precedes the conscious mental reports of decisions. The idea that we choose and then these choices are effected in the body must therefore be a *post-hoc* addition to the real physical basis of choice.

The Materialist View of Free Will

Materialists—who wish to explain away free will as an illusion—have jumped at these findings. They suggest that Libet's experiments demonstrate that consciousness is an epiphenomenon of neurons. Like fluidity arises from a molecular explanation of water, they claim that consciousness and free will are not real facts, but things that emerge out of neurological activity. In particular, there isn't anything *irreducible* or fundamental about free will. Indeed, if chemical activity in the brain precedes the conscious reports of choices, then the conscious reports are after-effects of the brain's chemical activity. A study of the chemical and biological activity in neurons would therefore lead us to an explanation of how these epiphenomena arise. Free will is then just a mistake of *retrospection* where we attribute ourselves free will and volition *after* the brain has already made its decision through chemical activity. Materialists now claim that consciousness and free will are part of our folk psychology in which we think of ourselves as different from ordinary material objects, but which does not have a scientific grounding in fact.

The Vedic Theory of Free Will

Before I delve into how Libet interpreted his experiments, I will describe the Vedic theory of volition and then compare Libet's view with the Vedic theory. In the Vedas, there are three aspects of consciousness—*dṛsta* (observer), *anumantā* (approver), and *puruṣa*

15

(enjoyer). Of particular relevance here is the *approver* aspect of consciousness. Consciousness, in the material world, does not generate ideas or thoughts. All ideas are generated from the *chitta*, which is the unconscious repository of impressions from past experiences. The *chitta* is capable of combining past experiences and producing new ideas. Thus, we can imagine a "golden mountain" by combining past impressions of "gold" and "mountain." The Vedas state that ideas are generated automatically from the *chitta*, without the intervention of consciousness. This production of ideas from the *chitta* is mediated by Time. For instance, if you usually exercise at some fixed time during the day, thoughts of exercising will automatically arise in your mind at that time. The impressions in the *chitta* carry the impression of the time in which they were earlier created. When the same type of time recurs, these thoughts are recreated. This view of causality requires a new view of time, which I will discuss later. Time, in this view, is semantic and cyclic rather than linear and physical. The notion of time is necessitated by some basic problems in science, which require the inclusion of meaning in matter.

Once thoughts have automatically been created by the *chitta* under the influence of Time, free will plays a role in *approving* or *disapproving* these thoughts. Consciousness approves a thought by keeping its attention on it. If consciousness withdraws the attention, the thought ceases to exist. In the Vedic view, thus, consciousness is the *existential* cause and not the *efficient* cause. That is, it does not produce the thoughts although it maintains these thoughts by choosing to be aware of them or kills them by withdrawing itself.

An *efficient* cause is one that acts to create an effect. An *existential* cause is one in whose presence the effect comes about, although the cause does not produce the effect. An example of an existential cause is a referee who oversees a football match. Although the referee does not cause the match, the match cannot happen in the referee's absence. The referee oversees the match and permits it to proceed under his or her supervision. Consciousness, similarly, in Vedic philosophy, allows thoughts by *approving* their existence. The essence of conscious free will is thus *existential* and not *efficient*.

Most scientific and even philosophical views in modern times view free will as an efficient cause. They claim that we have direct control over our bodies, which runs counter to the idea that nature is governed by some material laws. In the Vedic view, the material laws create propositions for consciousness to approve or disapprove. Conscious causality is the ability to reject what is being proposed, although not the ability to create new propositions.

Because free will is existential, *chitta* will create thoughts prior to their approval by consciousness. In fact, in the Vedic scheme of conscious control, there are five unconscious instruments that successively help develop a thought into a change and these are called *chitta*, *prakṛti, mahattattva, ahaṃkāra,* and *śakti.* These correspond to five stages called *thinking, feeling, willing, knowing,* and *acting.* The production of thoughts from the *chitta* is thinking. This thought has to be liked or disliked, which is called feeling. The thought has to be judged to be good, which is called willing. One then must find a plan to fulfill the willing, which is called knowing. And, finally, one must have the abilities to fulfill the plan, which is called acting. Each successive conscious activity has an unconscious counterpart that influences it. Beyond this unconscious are the choices of consciousness. If consciousness withdraws its attention at any stage, the development of the experience is arrested at that stage itself.

When we speak about free will in everyday conversations, we do it in the sense of *willing* whereby the thoughts in the mind are produced from the mind's will. But, in Vedic philosophy, the thoughts we become aware of are not the product of the conscious will. They are automatically produced from the unconscious. The conscious free will has no control over the production of thoughts, but it has control over the *continuance* of thoughts. While the history of impressions is unconscious and material, the *approver* of these stages is non-material. Libet's experiments—which observe brain activity before conscious reports of free will—have observed the effect of the *chitta*, which automatically generates thoughts.

To observe the brain state corresponding to the activity in the *chitta* and then claim that to be an indication that free will is false is to misunderstand the process of decision making. The Vedic theory of cognition explains Libet's experiments because decisions are presented for approval by consciousness. Their continued existence is due to the approval. If the approval is withdrawn, then they cease to exist.

Furthermore, in the cases of learned responses, where ethics, methodological and procedural knowledge has been mastered, the actual igniting of brain areas will be many, one after another.

Libet's Interpretation of Experimental Data

Libet did not consider his experiments to be a denial of free will, although he drastically restricted its scope. He called it the "power of veto" which is essentially correct from the Vedic standpoint if we equate this power with the non-material consciousness, which merely accepts or rejects the content already generated by the *chitta*. Libet's experiments did not study consciousness but the creation of thought, feeling, or will as a *proposal* in matter, which must be accepted or denied by consciousness. These experiments don't limit the scope of the non-material conscious free will, although they do tell us that under the material influence, the facts to which the non-material conscious free will can apply are restricted to the facts that the material unconscious instruments can generate.

Is the Vedic Theory Empirical?

Indeed, for the most part, due to a strong identification with our mental thoughts we generally acquiesce to the automatically created thoughts. Only people who have tried to practice sense control or mind control—where they deny the proposals automatically created due to unconscious habits—have a very good idea of this state.

Essentially, at the beginning of this practice, one tries to reject the ideas generated automatically but always falls prey to them. During the depressing moments that follow, introspection reveals that the person was "driven" into enjoyment against his own "will." This is essentially because of an intimate identification with the automatically arising thoughts. When presented with an alluring thought to which we are much attached, we find it hard to ignore it.

Those who have given up addictions know that the difference between the addicted and non-addicted states is that the mind dwells a lot more upon the thought when the person is addicted. Solutions to addiction are therefore nipping the thought in the bud by withdrawing awareness away from the thought. This could be achieved by focusing on other things. When addiction goes away, thoughts about the addiction may come and go, and consciousness does not dwell on them. Essentially, the identification with an addiction has to reduce so that thoughts don't live long enough to become desires, desires don't live long enough to become wills, and wills don't stay long enough to become plans, and finally, plans don't stay long enough to become actions. Consciousness can withdraw from the thought at any stage of the thinking, feeling, willing, planning, and acting process. If consciousness withdraws, the development of the thought is arrested at the stage at which the withdrawal occurs.

The neurological experiments that will prove the Vedic theory can be done on addicts, before and after their addiction. When the person is addicted, the brain firings will come before he says "yes" to that will. When the person is not addicted, the brain firings will still come, but now he will say "no" to them, after which the firings will cease to exist. In the first case, the neural firings lead to action and, in the latter, firings don't lead to action. Obviously, then, we must conclude that there must be something in between the neural firing and the action. That is the real free will of consciousness.

Since the free will—conditioned by past memories—always says "yes" to the unconsciously arising thoughts and desires, we tend to think that the brain pre-determines the conscious free will. When consciousness will say "no" to the created thoughts, then we will be able to distinguish between the brain and conscious free will. The brain firings are nothing but the effects of unconscious instruments called *chitta*, *prakṛti*, *mahattattva*, *ahaṃkāra* and *śakti* in Vedic philosophy. Conscious free will is, however, different from the unconscious. The Vedas state that if we are under a material influence, free will is not obvious. Free will is seen when consciousness begins to reject material allurements. If we want to observe the true free will of consciousness, then we must first create the conditions of true free will by giving up the identification with matter. When conscious free will go against the thoughts and desires generated by the unconscious impressions, then we can see that thoughts in the brain depend on the conscious free will, and not vice versa.

3

Evolution—Mind over Matter

Darwin's Evolutionary Theory

Every science begins with classification. We first want to identify commonalities underlying the diverse phenomena before we begin to generalize these commonalities into a theory of nature. The goal of biologists before Darwin was to achieve a success similar to the creation of the "periodic table" in chemistry. Like chemists put Helium, Neon, Argon, Krypton in the same class of "noble gases" because they are all chemically inert, biologists wanted to classify species of life into similar categories, based upon structure, behavior, eating and mating habits, migration, etc. Darwin too started out with a similar approach. He wanted to formulate insights such as "lions, tigers, and leopards belong to the cat family"—an approach that can be extended. We can say that all grains and pulses are varieties of grasses. Pumpkins and melons belong to the gourd family. Darwin found similarities between species based upon their habitat, their mating habits, fossils of bones, and the shape of their skulls.

But, like physicists are not content with saying that there are common classes of chemical elements, but want to seek out the origin of all the elements through a study of sub-atomic particles, Darwin too was not content with this classification. He wanted to seek out the "origins" of life—the common thing from which all life forms must have evolved. Biologists before him (such as Lamarck) had proposed two ideas that Darwin used: (1) the environment plays an important role in a species developing new traits, and (2) these traits can then be passed on to the offspring as native traits of the species. Mendel later found a genetic basis for Lamarckian ideas, thereby reinforcing them.

However, unlike Lamarck who thought that all evolution was based upon an individual effort (we can call it the *choice*) to adapt, Darwin discarded this freedom in the organism. According to Darwin, species are not free to adapt. Rather, the ones that don't adapt are eliminated. It is this idea that has subsequently been adopted by Social Darwinists for rationalizing things as diverse as capitalism, democracy, morality, and religion. In each case, the Darwinist argues, the social phenomenon imparts an evolutionary advantage for future survival. However, those that don't take the advantage would be eventually eliminated by the environment.

Molecular Evolutionary Theory

The modern evolutionary theory takes Darwin's ideas a step forward by basing them on molecular theories of genetics. Essentially, the idea is that a living being's genes hold the key to explaining all its physical traits and these genes undergo spontaneous "mutations" which can alter their molecular structure. As the mutated genes are passed on to the offspring, biological variety ensues. Some of these varieties survive because they are better adapted to the environment resulting in the propagation of genes while others perish, terminating that variety of genetic mutation. The generation of species in the modern evolutionary theory is therefore not based upon a *choice* to adapt but on spontaneous mutation. Genes randomly mutate and some of these mutations survive to create new species. The only thing needed to explain the diversity of species is the emergence of a molecule as complex as the DNA, which is now a problem of biochemistry and not biology proper. It is now hypothesized that complex molecules capable of replicating themselves emerged through random reactions over a long period of time. Whether there was enough time for such random reactions to produce a self-replicating system, is still a hotly debated topic in modern biology. Many people are prepared to grant that we can explain the *evolution* of a species, but we cannot explain the *origin* of species—which, as we all know, was the title of Darwin's book. Other critics say that evolution can explain minor variations to a species but cannot explain the emergence of fully functional diversity of species. Since these arguments are already well-documented in other places, I will not get into them here. I will rather present a different argument.

Problems with Evolutionary Theory

The foundation of evolutionary theory is random mutation followed by natural selection. Evolutionists argue that *when* a random mutation assists the survival of species, then the mutation becomes a long-lived feature of the species. The problem in this view is that in a stable ecosystem no single mutation can change the equilibrium unilaterally. Take, for example, the economic ecosystem made up of producers, consumers, distributors, and recyclers. If some producers decide to increase their production, the change can work only when there is a concerted change by the other players including distributors, consumers, and recyclers. If other ecosystem players don't change in concert, then increases in production cannot unilaterally be a source of benefit to the producer. In fact, the producer will have to halt the production after some time to drain their inventory.

Similarly, I can unilaterally stop paying taxes to increase my financial savings. But the only way lesser taxes will work is if there is lesser crime, disease, geopolitical uncertainty, and natural disasters. These will in turn put a lot of people involved with the government out of a job and will have to find alternative employment. They can only find alternative employment if there are demands for other kinds of things. The point is simply that no individual can unilaterally change in an ecosystem. The entire ecosystem has to change collectively because all the species are tied in a cycle of exchange.

Evolutionary data shows large gaps in fossil evidence. This is possible only if the ecosystem as a whole hops from one stable state to another. The big picture of evolution is large and sudden changes in the ecosystem and not continuous incremental change. The detailed picture of evolution is indeed small changes, but the small changes occur only after the big changes have taken place. The small changes are like an increase in the production of a type of product or service when the ecosystem has migrated to a new type of product or service.

Or, to a small increase or decrease in taxes after incremental improvements in healthcare or crime have been achieved. But, here too, should we say that the changes in the rate of production or the rate of taxation is an outcome of a random mutation or could it be an outcome of stabilizing after a big change?

Looking at the problem of fossil evidence gaps, some evolutionists have proposed a theory called *Punctuated Equilibrium* (PE) in which evolution happens in rapid bursts after which the ecosystem remains more-or-less the same for a few million years. Of course, this begs the question of *what* causes the rapid evolutionary change. PE attributes these changes to the environment, such as climate change, earthquakes, volcanic eruptions, etc. This pushes the biological explanation to changes in the environment. The problem of the diversification of the species is now a problem for the geologist or the weatherman. Then, why do we need random mutations and natural selection? Clearly, we won't seem to have a need for them.

The problem of evolution is that it treats random mutation as the main cause of change. This kind of mutation does not explain the large changes in an ecosystem. As a theoretical construct, it fails to explain persistent change, because the ecosystem will force a reversal unless most parts of the ecosystem change collectively. The observed facts about evolution can only be explained if we solve the big picture of change first. That means we need explanations of how the ecosystem as a whole evolves from one state to another. That mechanism cannot be random mutations. And when such a theory of large-scale change is available, it could then potentially also be used to understand the small changes. In such a theory, the cause is not random. Rather, there is a real explanation that we may not yet understand and which therefore appears to us as randomness.

The Vedic Theory of Evolution

In the Vedic view, bodies don't evolve although consciousness does. All kinds of bodies are available to a living being, much like various kinds of concepts, ideas and theories are available for adoption. Like we are free to be capitalists or communists, a living being can also choose a type of body because all matter is a possibility[1]. The adoption of a body is not qualitatively different from the adoption of an idea. However, the adoption of ideas and ideologies is governed by cycles in Time, in addition to individual activities and the results of these activities. Ideas and ideologies appear and disappear collectively in nature and this collective evolution of ideas and ideologies is governed by the cyclic progression in Time. This means that the same species will appear, disappear and reappear in time.

We noted in the previous article that consciousness does not create ideas. The ideas are created by Time and presented for approval to consciousness. Accordingly, the macroscopic trends of idea adoption (and appearance or disappearance of species) are under the influence of Time. Like there are cycles of economic boom and bust, social opulence and poverty, food abundance and famine, there is also the appearance and disappearance of bodies. This appearance and disappearance do not in any sense indicate the *creation* or *destruction* of species. Rather, as all ideas are always possible, but only appear or disappear at certain times, similarly, all species are always conceptually existent but appear and disappear due to the cyclic influences of time. Innate in this view is the idea that material objects are produced from meanings, and meanings are produced through choices. The appearance and disappearance of species, therefore, depends on the collective choices of the individuals and cycles in time. The fossils are telling us about the history of ideologies. They are a historical imprint of the collective ideological evolution.

In the Vedic view, a living being is accorded a body based upon its prior habits which are embedded in the unconscious. As the impressions in the unconscious evolve, the living being gets new kinds of bodies. This acquisition of a body based on habits is called transmigration. Of course, transmigration is subject to constraints of Time because an idea can only exist in the ecosystem of related ideas. While I might have a certain type of idea, I cannot maintain my existence based on that idea unless there are others who also believe in similar things. Ideas, therefore, do not appear in isolation. They rather appear collectively. The collection of ideas evolves under the cycles of Time.

---

1   The selection of a body is not a free choice and is governed by the past activities and the results of those actions. This is further elaborated later on.

Each species of life is essentially one kind of meaning of life and the common types of minds and bodies in that species are actually diversities of this common meaning of existence.

Can Semantic Evolution be Scientific?

A new theory of space and time is needed to formulate a semantic understanding of matter. The semantic view requires space to be closed and time to be cyclic[2]. Further, it requires both space and time to be defined hierarchically, similar to how we define postal addresses and clock times. The address of my house, for instance, includes the house number embedded inside the street address, the street address embedded inside the area name, the area inside a city, a city inside a state, a state inside a country, and so forth. Time similarly is described in cycles of seconds, minutes, hours, days, weeks, months, and years. Directions in space are given in terms of types such as East and West, while directions in time are understood in terms of past, present, and future where the future indicates 'progress' and the past indicates 'regress.' These semantic notions of space and time don't exist in modern science which treats space and time as an open and infinitely extended domain of objects.

Object names in a hierarchical space are not globally unique but unique only within the context of the next higher region. For instance, every large city in India has a "Mahatma Gandhi Road," which represents not a globally unique name, but only something unique in the city. A clock time, similarly, has a name unique within the context of the next higher duration. For instance, it is 11:00 AM every day and it is January 3rd every year. We define the location and duration through a relation to a larger location and duration, using part-whole relationships. While such relationships and semantic notions of space and

---

2   This point requires a level of detail that will take us outside the scope of this essay. The interested readers are referred to *Gödel's Mistake* for a detailed discussion for the rationale behind this idea. However, briefly, meanings are defined through a relation between a part and the whole, which are in turn defined through their relation to a larger whole. The definition of wholes in space requires space to be closed and time to be cyclic.

time are common in the everyday world, they have no role in current science. Hierarchical notions of space and time are semantic descriptions, because the names and meanings of locations and instances are given in relation to the whole.

A hierarchical theory of time is also a cyclic theory of time. Like the passing of days and nights, months, seasons, and years, only to return to the same type of event over and over again, a cyclic time will explain how nature evolves in cycles rather than linearly. In this cyclic movement, the entire region of closed space is transformed into a new state, rather than individual changes to each part that leave the other parts unchanged. This view about space and time dramatically affects current ideas about evolution.

For instance, the theory of evolution cannot speak about the random mutations in the individual species as the cause of macroscopic evolution. Rather, the theory must speak about the evolution of the ecosystem (a closed region of space) whose states change cyclically. Since the ecosystem evolves to new states, there is a role for natural selection to compel individual species to adapt to the large-scale changes. But it is not natural selection following random mutations. It is rather large-scale change percolating downward into small-scale changes. Random traits, in fact, will not even fit into the ecosystem, and they would be reversed by the rest of the ecosystem. The ecosystem cyclic evolution is a semantic evolution while the current theory based on random mutations is a physical theory.

The Scientific Need for Semantics

Hierarchical notions of space and time are necessary to solve the problems of semantics in mathematics, physics, computing, and many other areas of modern science. Problems of semantics appear in mathematics in the form of Gödel's Incompleteness. The problem appears in computing as Turing's Halting Problem. Problems of incompleteness in physical theories are problems related to collections of particles rather than individual particles and these problems can also be seen as problems of meaning within matter because meanings arise in collections rather than in individuals.

The solution to these problems requires a new view of matter, which in turn depends on a new view of space and time. I have extensively discussed problems of semantics in science and their possible solutions in my other books. *Gödel's Mistake* discusses the problems of meaning in mathematics and computing. *Quantum Meaning* discusses the problems in atomic theory. *Sāṅkhya and Science* surveys the implications of a semantic view for other fields in science such as chemistry, biology, linguistics, and psychology.

The modern theory of biological evolution is a materialistic theory based on views of mathematics, physics, and computing that do not incorporate meanings. Evolutionists take mathematics, physics, and computing in the current form to be the final theories, when, in fact, several fundamental problems remain unresolved. In 1900, Lord Kelvin famously proclaimed that physics was complete and all that remained were more precise measurements except for two main problems, namely black-body radiation and the constant speed of light. As we now know, these two problems led to quantum theory and general relativity. The problems that modern science faces today faces are, if anything, far more profound than in the past.

The problem of meaning is so pervasive and yet so completely ignored by science, that the problems of black-body radiation and the constant speed of light pale in comparison. When the problem of meaning will be solved, it will change the shape of science as we know it today. It will bring fundamental changes to our view of matter, space, time, change, and causality. It is only natural to suppose that it will also change the nature of biology and evolution.

Scientists often claim that the current materialistic view of nature will explain the origin of meanings, although it is well-known that attempts to incorporate meanings in mathematics and computing lead to logical paradoxes. This implies that we don't currently have a mathematical language in which meanings can be described. No amount of biological complexity will ever explain the mind unless meanings can be consistently incorporated in mathematics. The evolutionist's idea that materialistic theories will explain the mind is therefore flawed. This does not necessarily imply that there is no evolution. Rather, we require a semantic version of evolution in which living bodies evolve in a way similar to the evolution of ideas, ideologies, cultures, and societies. These evolutions require semantic notions of space and time, which are possible if space and time are described as closed, cyclic, and hierarchical constructs.

In brief, there is biological evolution in nature, but it does not use random mutations or natural selection and does not represent incremental progress. The evolution is cyclic, evolves the ecosystem as a whole, and is governed by laws of meaning. Living beings in this evolution are bodies developed on top of minds. A species is a type of mind before it is a type of body. The evolution of the body, too, is therefore governed by the laws of the evolution of ideas.

Material Functionalism

A cornerstone of biological evolution is the idea that material complexity leads to some *functional* systems. For instance, our bodies are comprised of many parts—hands, legs, stomach, head, chest, etc. The body is also internally divided into many functional systems such as digesting, breathing, circulation, elimination, etc. In the modern theory of biological evolution, it is supposed that the complexity of the biological functions is an accident of nature. These are not *fundamental*; they are rather *emergent* properties of the parts.

In fact, biology postulates a direct dependence between *structure* and *function*. If you have a molecule of a certain type, you will get the necessary function. This claim is false because a molecule doesn't react with every other molecule, just like one cell in the body doesn't interact with every other molecule. The selective interaction between molecules and cells is itself functionalism. The structure doesn't determine which two molecules or cells will interact. The same parts can interact in different ways, creating new functions. So, the first important thing to note is that structure and function are different things, and one doesn't reduce to the other. The second important thing is that even if structure emerges through mutations, the same cannot be said about function, because the interaction between two things has no material counterpart. Which part will interact causally with which other parts is not decided by the parts.

Furthermore, the random aggregation of parts will also create two types of dysfunctional systems—if we look upon them information-ally or programmatically. First, they will constitute programs that will crash. Second, they will constitute programs that will run forever. Alan Turing proved a famous theorem (called the Halting Problem) show-ing that there is no mechanical procedure capable of eliminating pro-grams that run forever. In evolution, we can suppose the programs that crash to be living beings who are just not well-suited to live in the environment. But evolution will also produce programs that run for-ever which corresponds to living beings who never die. Since there is no mechanical procedure (such as natural selection) to eliminate such eternal beings, if such beings were ever produced accidentally then they would live on forever. I call this Evolution's Halting Problem and it is described in my book entitled *Signs of Life: A Semantic Critique of Evolutionary Theory*.

It is thus not enough to suppose that randomness will create living beings. It is also necessary to explain why all living beings die. The beings that die are finite programs. Randomly created programs can however be infinite. To avoid this, it is necessary to identify the mean-ings such that only meaningful programs will run in nature. If the pro-gram is meaningful, then meanings must exist prior to the program. This issue about program semantics is discussed at length in *Gödel's Mistake*. The functional viewpoint therefore naturally leads us to the problems of semantics, in which the program design and its purpose must exist logically prior to the program.

If we take a living being as a logical system, the inconsistency and incompleteness imply that either the functional system will have parts that act at cross-purposes (inconsistency) or it will have parts that cannot perform some essential functions necessary to form a system (incompleteness). These two problems imply that there cannot be a logically consistent functional system, because there is no mathe-matical language in which such systems can be described. In so far as nature is mathematically governed, logically contradictory things cannot exist. In so far as biology is the study of functional bodies, functionally incomplete bodies cannot exist. Readers are referred to *Gödel's Mistake* for a discussion of program semantics and to *Signs of Life* for its implications in biology.

The key conclusion from these illustrations is that if nature begins in *a priori* real particles which then aggregate to represent meanings, then there can never be a consistent or complete theory of nature. There can however be a consistent and complete theory if the wholes are divided into parts, rather than aggregating the independent parts into a whole. Thus, if there are functions in nature, then wholes must exist logically prior to the parts. The functional role of a part is not an additional property of logically independent parts, but due to the relation between the whole and the parts.

The idea that wholes exist logically prior to the parts creates some difficulties in our understanding of nature. In what form does the whole exist when there are no parts? This problem can be solved if both whole and part are concepts. The whole is a summarized concept and the parts detail that concept. Material objects develop from ideas, and the body develops from the mind. Initially, these ideas exist in a summarized form and constitute the wholes. As further information is added, the same information is detailed thereby creating multiple parts. This viewpoint has implications for many areas of science, including physics, mathematics, computing, linguistics, and biology. I have described these in *Sāṅkhya and Science*.

4

Intelligent Design and Vedic Philosophy

What Is Creationism?

Creationism is the idea that the universe was created by an intelligent being: God, and that it emerged not slowly, through stages lasting millions of years—as biological and Darwinian evolution currently demands—but all at once. God's intervention in the act of universal creation can however be construed in many ways.

First, we can say that God controls changes in the universe directly, and every change in the world is effected by God's will. Not even a blade of grass moves without God's approval. This view creates the problem of free will; for instance, if God controls all changes then does it mean that we don't have free will? And if we don't have free will, then why would we be accountable for our actions?

Second, we can say that God does not control all changes but He creates matter and its laws which in turn control the world. God, in this view, does not create the galaxies, planets, and species. These are created by the natural laws. However, God *tuned* matter and its laws such that they would permit the existence of living beings. This view equates nature with what science has discovered but attributes the fine-tuning of natural constants (such as the strength of the gravitational pull or the speed of light) to God's design. Some creationists claim that species are created by evolution *after* God has tuned the laws. The problem is still that the laws of physics do not permit free will. While inducting a role for God in nature, the view does not permit a clear role for mind and consciousness in the universe. This view will also, therefore, carry forward all the problems of meaning and incompleteness that exist in current theories of science.

31

Third, we can say that God creates matter, its laws, and all the things and species in the universe but these laws are different from the ones that science has currently discovered. Current scientific laws are laws about the motion of matter and not moral laws of choice and meaning. When God creates the universe, He creates matter, meaning, and moral laws. The living beings are free to choose, but their choices have consequences. The relation between choice and consequence is a moral law; it includes physical laws but goes beyond them. The big problem with this view is that we still don't know what these laws are, how they act on matter, and why they seem different from what science has so far discovered.

What Is Intelligent Design?

Intelligent Design (ID) is a form of creationism (although different from Christian creationism where the universe is a few thousand years old) in which the laws of nature do not determine everything. Specifically, they do not determine the formation of species, as the laws are compatible with many material configurations, not all of which can be living. To fix this indeterminism, God provides design in the creation. This design exists as structure and function in matter. The *mechanism* by which God embeds this design is, however, not understood. For instance, structure and function are properties of material objects in space and time. How does God interact with the material objects in space and time? What forms of causality should we construe to explain this interaction? ID is based on the realization that there is considerable complexity in living beings, which could not have arisen through random mutations[3].

The Vedic View of Creation

In the Vedic view, which I describe at length in *Six Causes*, the universe begins in the choices of consciousness which produce a *language*

---

3   The reader is referred to the works of Stephen C. Meyer, Michael Behe, Rupert Sheldrake and Thomas Nagel.

of symbols called *śabda-brahmān*. This language has many kinds of *meanings* much like words have many meanings. These include concepts in the mind, judgments in the intelligence, intentions in the ego, and morality in a 'conditioned' consciousness called *mahattattva*. The alphabets of this language are objectified as symbols in Ether. As more and more meanings are added to Ether, matter becomes more and more 'dense' and produces other elements such as Air, Fire, Water, and Earth. These elements are not the ordinary things called by those names, but objectifications of information in the form of sound, touch, sight, taste, and smell. The aspect of this viewpoint that is relevant to the question of ID is the idea that material objects are created by objectifying meanings in matter.

The objectification creates symbols which are material objects, but their meanings depend on the space-time structure. The space-time properties make these symbols representations of meaning. For instance, different locations in space denote concepts and the order of these concepts in time constructs a proposition. A proposition is not a pre-existing object written in matter like a sentence in a book. It is rather produced in time by ordering concepts, much like speech produces sentences through a succession of words. When we read a sentence, we can say that all the words exist simultaneously in the book. But when we hear a sentence, we can only say that the proposition is objectified into space-time symbols in time.

Vedic Creationism and Intelligent Design

ID theorists claim that design is injected by a creator. In Vedic philosophy, 'design' is a subtle material reality that exists as meanings in a 'subtle' body comprising mind, intelligence, ego, and *mahattattva*. These meanings are converted into 'gross' matter which we can observe. The structure and function in matter owe their origin to meanings in the subtle body. Since these meanings are prior to the body, the evolutionary idea that meanings are *emergent* properties of random chance mutations in matter is false from the Vedic standpoint. Meanings in the Vedic view are fundamental and it is matter that is emergent. The causality in matter is, therefore, based on the meanings and not based on physical properties.

A living being—the Vedas describe—enters a specific type of mother's womb at a specific time based on its subtle body which carries impressions, desires, and *karma* from its previous lives. Thus, a species is defined not by the body but by meanings. It is the mind that is the dog, the cat, the horse, or the human being. The mind *expresses* these meanings into the body, thereby creating a body suitable for the mind. Note that the body is, in this view, only a medium of communicating the meanings in the mind to other minds. To the extent that the mind wishes to communicate with other minds—and needs to objectify the meanings from the mind into the body—the living being needs a body besides the mind. The body, therefore, is not the origin of the meanings, but rather the *expression* of meanings that already existed in the subtle body of the living being.

The 'design' in ID is therefore not generated by God directly in Vedic philosophy. It is rather a subtle level of material reality present in the subtle body of every living being. This subtle body produces a gross body of structure and functions. Of course, God does create the primordial language of meanings, but to create a specific type of thing or concept, these meanings have to be used by consciousness. The choices of meanings create a specific *type* of mind which in turn produces a specific type of body. While God is the creator of the primordial meanings, He is not the creator of the *objects*. The objects are produced from the history of a living being.

The law of nature in Vedic philosophy involves both effects and consequences. An *effect* of a choice is the immediate outcome, such as the bullet being shot by the pulling of a trigger. A consequence is the *reaction* to the choice, which comprises three things. First, there is a moral judgment of whether the act was right or wrong. Second, an unconscious impression of the action is formed which creates a bias in the living entity about what is true and false; the false things are defocused while the biased view of truth is focused upon. Third, every action shapes a living entity's personality of desires, likes, and dislikes, or what kind of situation he or she feels comfortable in. When the soul is injected into a mother's womb, the living entity carries this subtle body of moral consequences, impressions, and personality. From this body, the morality, ego, intellect, mind, senses, and the body are developed gradually. What we see therefore is produced from what remains unconscious for most people.

Modern science studies only the *effects* and completely neglects the consequences which are the cause of subsequent bodies. Even the effects are studied based on physical properties rather than on the meanings. If there are no meanings, then there are no judgments of truth, good, and right, and hence there are no consequences. So, the theoretical framework of science preempts many types of causes. But all of these are material and not actions of God. The so-called 'design' is the living entity itself; he or she is designing their own body as a result of consequences created in the past.

A Different Material Science

I have discussed the Vedic theory of action, effect, and consequence in my other book entitled *Moral Materialism*, which also discusses the debate between free will and determinism. The book discusses two kinds of laws—(1) that determine the cosmic space-time structure of events, which are deterministic, and (2) the trajectory or the succession of events for a given observer in the universe. The cosmic events are predetermined, like the script of a drama that has been previously authored, although the drama hasn't yet been enacted. The succession of events of an individual observer is governed by the role governed by the consequences of one's previous actions. The soul has limited free will to reject what is being produced by the material machinery and thereby withdraw its consciousness, as we saw in a previous essay. Sometimes, this withdrawal causes a change in the observer's experiences, and sometimes they don't. Hence, there is an explicit role for both consequences and choices.

The brief overview of these ideas above illustrates that adding the notion of design into matter will only address the gap between the physical and the biological complexities without an explanation of how this design is embedded in matter. Morever, this approach will not explain the existence of mind and meaning in nature. Physical theories cannot explain the mind. Therefore, even if we did postulate an element of design, we will still have to postulate another explanation for the mind. If God provides the design in matter, but that design influences our thinking, feeling, and other psychological states, then

God's will would seem to interfere with the living being's free will and thus lead to other problems of mind and choice.

The Vedic approach is more sophisticated because it attributes design to the living being's rather than to God's mind. The body of a living being arises as a consequence of its choices, not the will of God. This, however, requires a more drastic adjustment to our notions about matter than entailed by ID. In ID, matter is adequately described by current laws of nature. The laws of nature underdetermine the complexity which is bridged by God's design. In the Vedic view, however, the complexity is bridged by the living being's past. The laws that govern the evolution of an observer's experiences are the laws of choice. Their consequences create both the body and the mind. The causality, therefore, goes beyond current science.

ID tells us that there is a gap between the current physical account and reality. ID then attributes this difference to the fine-tuning of nature and to the use of design. The fine-tuning and design require a designer, which is not the living entity whose body is being designed. In Vedic philosophy, the physical theory is not even partially true. The theory based on meaning is partially true. Deeper than these meanings are the unconscious consequences of previous actions. And deeper than these are the choices made by the living entity. So, the creation of the body and the mind, and their successive experiences, involves far more complexity than ID postulates.

Design and Material Science

In short, what ID calls 'design' is a subtle form of material reality in Vedic philosophy. It is incorrect to think that there are independent material objects which then combine to produce living beings and the combination of objects is design. It is rather more correct to think that the design precedes matter and creates material objects with the right kind of intention, structure, and function. Hence, there is design because matter is produced from subtle meanings.

ID aims to explain the emergence of biological complexity without explaining how the mind works. A molecular mechanism—regardless of its sophistication—cannot explain the mind unless the atoms are themselves representations of ideas, like words—as material objects—are symbols of meanings. In fact, the problems of meaning are much more profound than the problems of biological complexity because the problems of meaning appear even in mathematics, physics, and computing, whereas the problem of biological complexity appears only in biology. If we try to solve the problem of biological complexity without solving the problem of meaning, we will require another set of mechanisms that can explain the mind, and these problems cannot be solved without a fundamental revision to our notions about matter, space-time, and numbers. On the other hand, once the problem of meaning has been solved in physics, mathematics, and computing, a separate solution to the problem of biological complexity would be quite unnecessary. Therefore, the solution of biological complexity using the idea of ID does not solve the problem of meaning although the solution to the problem of meaning also addresses the problem of biological complexity.

Design indicates that the current physical theories do not explain biological complexity. However, since this complexity cannot be explained by any other natural process in science, the ID theorist attributes it to God. But even if we attribute design to God, we would not have solved the problem of mind, which are obviously natural, although not reducible to current physical theories of matter.

The problem of the mind requires a different theory of matter. And when this theory is present, the idea that information is encoded in matter as God's design will not be necessary. ID is only an indication of the problem and not of the real solution. A semantic theory of nature is the solution, and although it does not require transcendent causes, it certainly needs a new theory of matter.

5

Impersonalism, Voidism and Science

Einstein's Religion

Einstein once said that "If there is a religion that could correspond to the needs of science, it would be Buddhism." Why Buddhism? That is because in Buddhism there is no soul or God. The ultimate reality is a void, which would resonate with the scientific idea that the universe springs from a space-time vacuum. In Einstein's theory of relativity, matter emerges from the *curvature* in space-time, and to produce matter, curvature has to be added to space-time. Similarly, in atomic theory, quantum particles are created from the fluctuations of a vacuum. These fluctuations cannot, at present, be predicted, although the theory says they are probable. How this probability becomes a reality requires the addition of something that does not presently exist within science (the standard interpretation of quantum theory requires a collapse postulate that converts the probabilities into reality). There are hence many New Age philosophies which begin by supposing a vacuum of space-time along with a universal quantum wavefunction from which the universe springs. This kind of religion is impersonalistic or voidistic, but it gels well with the scientific materialism, and hence some religiously inclined people—like Einstein—suppose that these may be the meeting point between religion and science, not the ones that postulate God.

What Are Impersonalism and Voidism?

In the personalist religions—which postulate that God is a person— the form in nature is produced by God. There are different variations of this idea, some in which God is the creator of form (such as Abrahamic religions), and others (such as Vedic philosophy) in which form emerges from the body of God in the act of self-consciousness. Regardless of how you suppose the form is produced, its cause is traced back to an original Being. Modern science has considerable problems with postulating such a Being because it stemmed from a conflict with religion—especially the Abrahamic religions. Conversely, the idea that form can emerge from the formless is much more acceptable in science, because it requires no God. This is precisely the reason why scientists are attracted to the philosophies of impersonalism and voidism, which claim that the ultimate reality is formless, and forms are emergent and temporary effects.

When reality is identified as formless space-time and the universal quantum wavefunction, all forms that emerge from this are fleeting, and that goes well with the idea that the material world is ever-changing and not eternal. The reality is something from which it is produced, and therefore the phenomena are illusions. Impersonalism and voidism claim that the ultimate reality is *formless*. Impersonalism claims that ultimate reality is a non-dual 'substance' in which the duality of form does not exist. Voidism claims that the ultimate reality is nothingness, in which the non-dual substance is also discarded. While impersonalism regards the non-dual reality as consciousness, voidism denies even the existence of consciousness. In voidism, there is no experiencer beyond the experience. Both the experiencer and the experience are created simultaneously.

In recent times, many attempts to bring science and religion together have been motivated from the impersonalist and voidist philosophical stances. Buddhism is a philosophy of voidism while *Advaita Vedanta* is a philosophy of impersonalism. On the face of it, there is tremendous synergy between science and these ideologies of formlessness because science too tries to describe the ultimate reality as a formless vacuum. In both cases, forms are emergent rather than fundamental properties of nature. However, once you acknowledge that ultimate reality is formless, it hardly matters whether you call it space-time, nothingness, or oneness. These are more or less equivalent formulations of the same basic idea.

A History of Impersonalism and Voidism

In Indian philosophy, impersonalism (the idea that there is an ultimate formless reality) arose in the philosophy of the great savant *Sankarāchārya* who produced an interpretation of *Vedanta Sutra* (the summarized conclusions of the Vedas) arguing that Brahman is real while this world is unreal. Impersonalists quote the Vedantic aphorism: *brahma satyam jagat mithya*, implying that Brahman is real while the manifest universe of differentiated forms is unreal. Since the experience of the individuality of observers is also part of the worldly experiences, the impersonalist claims that the distinction between observers is false. There is hence only a single existence that is segregated into many observers and their experiences, and this separation is an illusion. Only the single existence that existed prior to the creation of many observers is therefore real.

Sankarāchārya's impersonalism was a response to the inroads Buddhism was making in Indian society around 8ᵗʰ century AD. Buddhism had criticized the rampant ritualism (often without a profound philosophical grounding) prevalent in Indian society at that time. But in thus criticizing the Vedic religion, Buddhism gradually undermined the authority of the Vedas themselves. Centuries later, *Sankarāchārya* revived the Vedic religion's philosophy, restoring the authority of the Vedas, although he also rejected the practices of rituals. His work led to a new interpretation of *Vedanta Sutra*, in which ultimate reality is conceived as being formless and impersonal.

Buddhism had claimed that both the observer and the observed are unreal, and to know 'reality' one must know the emptiness in which neither subject nor object is real. *Sankarāchārya* reinstated the existence of a transcendental subject without rescuing the material world from non-existence. But how much better is the undivided oneness of a transcendental observer than the emptiness of space-time is questionable. If you cannot use distinctions, you cannot use language. It may not mean that oneness and nothingness are unreal. However, it does mean that we cannot *speak* about them using language in the conventional sense because every word or sound represents a form, and the referred object must have a form.

Compare impersonalism and voidism with modern science. Here, only matter is real and the observers, although conscious, are also material. In the thinking about observers today, consciousness is an attribute of brains. Although what makes the brain conscious is still not known, the belief is that this ideology, when pursued, will give us the answers. Both observers and the phenomena they observe in science are this-worldly and not other-worldly. Furthermore, matter is not fundamental. Rather, the differences between objects are produced from an undifferentiated space-time. What causes their production remains an unsolved problem in science.

There is hence a considerable philosophical synergy between the ideas of impersonalism, voidism, and materialism in modern science. However, this similarity between these three viewpoints also implies that they inherit the common problem of converting the formless into something with form. The formless is undivided and undifferentiated while things with form are divided and differentiated. The problem of form can therefore also be stated as the problem of how a singular reality becomes differentiated into individual objects with form. Only when reality is differentiated can be it known, spoken about, and described in language. Materialism, impersonalism, and voidism do not explain the advent of form.

The similarities between voidism (where the ultimate reality is a void or nothingness), impersonalism (where the ultimate reality is an undifferentiated oneness), and scientific materialism (where the ultimate reality is space-time), have prompted some scientists (e.g., Einstein) and New Age spiritualists (e.g., Deepak Chopra) to see these parallels as avenues for reconciling the materialism in science with the mysticism in religions. These attempts at reconciliation however can get very confusing for many scientists and spiritualists alike. For instance, if reality is ultimately formless and living beings are accidents of the conversion of formlessness into form, then the practice of religion is an accident of nature as well. Why would we treat the religious experience as something profound if we do not treat the mundane experiences as being equally profound?

The Problem of Impersonalism and Voidism

The central difficulty in the philosophies of impersonalism and voidism is the inability to explain *how* the manifest world of forms is

41

created from the formless. For instance, if the universe prior to creation is oneness, then how is that oneness divided into many parts? If the universe is emptiness prior to creation, then what converts that emptiness into objects? The scientific counterpart of these questions is: If space-time is the fundamental entity from which the universe springs, then what causes the random fluctuation in that space-time, which, in turn, causes the manifest universe? Without such an explanation, the theory of nature is *incomplete* because it cannot explain the origin of form from the formless. It is not sufficient to say that there is a *mechanism* by which something can happen. It is also necessary to provide the cause that employs the mechanism. Random fluctuations are a mechanism by which form can be created. But without a cause that triggers them, the answer is incomplete.

In recent times, there have been attempts to solve this problem by postulating consciousness as a transcendent entity that creates the forms. For instance, some New Age thinkers claim that nature is a quantum probability wavefunction that consciousness collapses into definite states out of its choices. This consciousness, the spiritualist claims, is an impersonal cosmic consciousness, the field of choices in which the world of experience is created. But this idea of a cosmic impersonal consciousness is a misnomer because the idea of choice and the idea of oneness are incompatible; choices imply individuality, and if consciousness can choose, then it must be an individual. Choices without individuality cannot exist, because choice will have no disposition—i.e. how to choose one over the other? The idea of cosmic conscious choices thus leads to *inconsistency*. However, without the notion of a transcendent consciousness, there is no explanation for the emergence of form from the formless. In that scenario, the scientific explanation of nature is *incomplete*.

Science is already being stalked by problems of incompleteness and inconsistency which spirituality is supposed to solve. For, if science was already complete and consistent, then there would be no need for a spiritual alternative. By adopting impersonal and voidistic approaches, however, we again inherit problems of inconsistency and incompleteness, this time from the spiritual philosophy.

It has become customary in science to attribute anything that the scientific theory cannot explain to *randomness*. Thus space-time can randomly produce particles, and these randomly created particles can randomly combine to form complex molecules, which can randomly combine to produce living beings. By injecting the idea of randomness into a logical-empirical explanation of nature, such theories violate the fundamental goal in science which is to provide predictable cause-effect relationships and predictions. Those who propose randomness as an explanation of currently unexplained facts believe that they are proposing a unique scientific idea, but a closer look reveals that they are proposing infinite unique ideas.

Most impersonalist and voidist religious philosophies ride on this dogmatic approach to science. Just as matter can 'emerge' from the collapse of the wavefunction or changes to the geometry of space-time in physical theories, impersonalism and voidism suggest that forms are created from something formless. While claiming to provide a 'synthesis' of science and religion, in so far as the problem about the conversion of the formless to form is concerned, we would not have moved an inch in neither religion nor science. Religion just becomes an unnecessary addendum to science because it provides no logical value in terms of formulating new scientific theories.

Form and Personalism

There is another school of Indian philosophy—much older than both Buddhism and impersonalism—that provides a radically different view of creation. In this view, there are two things—matter and consciousness—which combine to create the universe. Both have the same type of form, comprising of three aspects. We have discussed the three aspects of the soul as *sat, chit*, and *ananda* earlier. The same form is also reflected in matter, producing three categories of material reality that correspond to the three aspects of the soul. Our conscious experiences and the material phenomena are the outcome of the separation of these forms followed by their combination. For example, in the case of matter, these three forms are cognition, emotion, and relation. The term 'cognition' represents all the concepts that build the body and the mind. The term 'emotion' refers to a material personality that gives rise to desires, likes, dislikes, etc. The term 'relation' refers to the roles these objects play contextually.

However, there is also a primordial state of both matter and consciousness in which these three aspects are not differentiated. In this state, consciousness exists as *oneness* and matter exists as *nothingness*. In the state of oneness, the different individual souls are not differentiated from each other—i.e. they are not *conscious* of their distinction from each other. They just exist without awareness of their individuality. Similarly, in the state of nothingness, the forms in matter are not differentiated; just like zero is the sum of all opposites, and yet the opposites exist inside zero, similarly, the duality of material nature is reconciled in the state of nothingness. These are also called the *unmanifest* state of matter and consciousness.

The philosophy of impersonalism corresponds to the undifferentiated state of consciousness and the philosophy of voidism corresponds to the undifferentiated state of matter. They are both acknowledged in Vedic philosophy, but they are not considered the ultimate reality because there is another transcendent reality, which is always manifest, although it is non-dual—i.e. not comprised of oppositions. The undifferentiated state of consciousness is called *Brahman* and the undifferentiated state of matter is called *Pradhāna*. In the manifest state, *Brahman* becomes the numerous individual souls aware of their individuality. Similarly, in the manifest state, *Pradhāna* is called *Prakriti* comprising three modes of nature.

Therefore, in one sense, the forms emerge from the formless. But in another sense, these forms were preexisting although the three modes of nature were coalesced into *Pradhāna* and the numerous individual souls were unaware of their individuality. The philosophies of impersonalism and voidism are not false, but they are theories about existence prior to the manifestation of the material world. The main reason these are not considered supreme is that there is a transcendent nature in which these forms exist in a manifest form. So, if you call the unmanifest reality as the supreme existence, you are right in terms of the origin of the material world, but wrong in the ultimate sense of what lies beyond matter.

This school of thought is sometimes called the personalist school in Indian philosophy because each soul is an individual. The individuality simply means that there is a predisposition toward choices. So, every soul has a *form*, which constitutes its original personality from which spring desires, likes, and dislikes. These in turn dictate the choices the soul makes, and they can be called its *free will*. However, the nature of free will is that you can suspend or surrender it. In the transcendent world, this free will is surrendered to God, so even though free will exists, it is subordinated to the free will of God. In the *Brahman* state, the free will is suspended, i.e. not used, and the soul becomes unaware of its individuality. This doesn't mean that the soul is no longer an individual. It is just that it is *unaware* of its individuality, not using its free will to make conscious decisions.

This suspension of free will is different from the illusion of free will. If there is free will to begin with, then it can be suspended to create oneness. But if there is no free will then it cannot be created from oneness. If individuality is fundamental, then it can create oneness. But if oneness is fundamental then it cannot create individuality. In the personalist school, therefore, individuality is said to be fundamental, from which oneness is created when the living being chooses to discard its own free will. The idea of free will is not reducible, neither to matter nor to an undivided being. It cannot be reduced to matter because free will can create *new* ideas while matter cannot produce anything new; matter can only be transformed from one state to another. Since free will can produce new information, while matter cannot, free will cannot be material.

While a living being may temporarily suspend its free will, and thereby merge into the oneness of a unified existence, this free will remains an innate property that can spring forth at any time. The state of oneness is therefore temporary, while free will is eternal. If you have free will you can give it up. But if you don't have free will you cannot create it. The paradox of form in impersonalism, voidism, and materialism cannot be solved because they attempt to create form from formless. The personalist view postulates that form exists as individual conscious beings whose free will is the *symptom* of their individuality. A conscious being chooses to become conscious of the world and can also withdraw from the world. The impersonalist notion of an impersonal and formless consciousness that is devoid of free will (and individuality) is therefore a misnomer. All conscious beings must have a form although by suspending that individuality, a soul can be merged into a formless existence.

Forms and Choices

Every form is therefore eternal however it may not always be manifest. These forms are manifest due to choices. Choices individuate a formless existence into a person and then objectify this personality into self-identity, intents, concepts, sensations, and things. The living being is said to be 'caught' in the material world, but this world is compared to a 'web' that the spider has produced out of itself. Through its choices, the living being encages itself into a material identity, intelligence, mind, senses, and finally a material body. The impersonalists jump at this problem and claim that since the root of the problem is the use of free will, we must discard the free will and merge into a single, undivided, undifferentiated, oneness.

The personalist however claims that the free will cannot be discarded. It can temporarily be suspended, but it will rise again and encage the living being *unless* it is used in a new way. Spirituality in Vedic philosophy begins with the idea that there are uses of free will that do not encage it. While a detailed description of this use of free will is out of the scope of this book, the fundamental point that I wanted to make here is that the forms in nature are not emergent properties. They are rather an eternal fundamental property. Form can be suspended when free will is suspended and the world returns to being formless. But form cannot be created from the formless. Ideas about formlessness in impersonalism, voidism, and materialism have a challenge on their hands—namely to explain the emergence of form from the formless. Postulating that form is created due to randomness in nature cannot be regarded as an explanation.

We can pretend that randomness is a scientific idea, but such theories will in the future be superseded by others that actually describe form in new ways. The next article discusses the relation between form and science and how ideas about form can and will transform science in unprecedented ways. The key takeaway from here, that I wish to highlight, is that impersonalism and voidism add nothing to science that science is not already doing through its materialist ideology. Impersonalism and voidism are pseudo-spiritual reinterpretations of the materialist philosophy in science. Do we really need them to augment science? I *personally* don't think so.

The personalist approach appears to be much more interesting, because it indicates that all form is eternal, but it exists in an unmanifest form. In a modern terminology, we can say that form exists as a *possibility* from which a reality is created by choice. We cannot observe this possibility *qua* possibility, and therefore it appears that the world is formless because it is not being observed. We can however explain the emergence of form from the possibility. Similarly, the universe of objects is dissolved into an undifferentiated material existence when consciousness stops its conscious choices[4].

When form is destroyed, the objects are unmanifest and cannot be known. However, since the soul is never destroyed, it can create form again. The total amount of matter when the universe is manifest is equal to the total amount of matter when the universe does not exist. The difference between the existence and non-existence of the universe is the total amount of information that is added to undifferentiated matter to produce a cosmos of individual objects. Choices are therefore responsible not for the creation of the world, but for differentiating the preexisting world into phenomena.

If information is the byproduct of randomness in emptiness, we wouldn't be able to causally explain the origin of information. If information originally exists in matter, and consciousness experiences it, then we would not be able to explain why information is semantic. It is only when information originates in consciousness and is then objectified in matter, that we can causally explain the origin of information as well as why this information must be semantic.

---

4   This claim might prompt some readers to ask: Does the universe disappear or become unmanifest when I close my eyes? In Vedic philosophy, even when we are unaware of the existence of the world, there is a form of God called *Paramātma* who continuously observes (and thus *maintains*) the universe by observation. The universe is annihilated when this form of God withdraws His consciousness. This is further detailed in the book *Six Causes*.

6

Why God's Existence Is a Scientific Question

Dawkins's Challenge

Richard Dawkins in his book *The God Delusion* presents a three-step argument for the non-existence of God. First, he claims that a universe made by God would be different from the universe created by natural occurrences. Second, he claims that our universe fits better with the idea that it is a product of natural occurrences than with the idea of a God as its creator. Third, he concludes that since our universe is more compatible with the idea of natural causes than with the idea of God, we are dealing with a naturalistic rather than a theistic universe. Dawkins's point is that if God exists, then this must make some *observable* difference to the nature of reality. If there is no observable difference, then God cannot be rationally confirmed or denied from the facts we can observe in the world. In such a scenario, God's existence is subject to Occam's razor—i.e. not multiplying entities beyond necessity—and can be discarded as a superfluous hypothesis. Now, we can conclude that God does not exist.

I personally think this is a great argument because it forces us to think about the implications the existence of God has in terms of observable facts in the material world. Of course, religious thought claims that God does make a difference in the world, intervening through His grace and performing miracles that violate well-known laws of science. But unless we understand how God intervenes in the world, such effects may also be attributed to material causes. After all, everything that happens in nature is *possible* naturally. God doesn't create something impossible or create something that could never be created by natural means. So, the question is only whether God caused something, or was it caused by natural means. To argue one way or another, one would need to understand how God intervenes in nature, and how He could cause anything if at all.

Richard Dawkins's argument is correct if the science of today is indeed the final picture of reality because this picture of nature defines a notion of causality that would make any causal connection between God and nature impossible. However, I don't think that current science is the final picture of reality. All areas of science—including mathematics, computing, physics, linguistics, and biology—suffer from problems of incompleteness, indeterminism, and uncertainty, which make it clear that physical notions of causality are insufficient. The analysis of these problems—which I have discussed in my other books—reveals that they can be solved if reality is treated as symbols representing meanings rather than as things. All symbols are things, but not all things are symbols. The incompleteness of current science thus indicates a flaw in our current theories which describe a nature of meanings as meaningless things. This flaw will remain a permanent limitation of science unless its foundations are revised. If, however, the scientific foundations are revised thereby inducting a fundamental role for meaning in nature, then this will also change the explanation of the universe's origin.

Now, we would ask: What is the origin of all meanings? If nature is physical and meanings are emergent properties of physical aggregations, then there is no role for God in the universe. However, if nature is semantic, and meanings are fundamental (rather than emergent) properties, which in turn produce material objects, then there is a very important role for God in the universe: the role is that God would now be the origin of all meanings. He would, in fact, be described as a primordial or the most abstract meaning from which other contingent or detailed meanings are produced. The existence of God, therefore, makes a difference to the scientific study of nature. The difference is that if God exists then nature would be described as symbols of meaning rather than as meaningless things.

In Vedic philosophy, God is described as the combination of six original meanings—knowledge, beauty, power, fame, wealth, and detachment. To just take one of these for illustration, there are many kinds of knowledge in this world, but we assume something called *knowledge* itself. How is knowledge itself different from a specific form of knowledge—e.g. physics? Similarly, there are many kinds of beauties but what is beauty itself, apart from its manifestations? Just like modern science postulates physical properties such as mass and charge, but at some point, we must ask: What is mass? What is charge? Similarly, if we study matter in terms of meanings, then we will arrive at primordial meanings, and we will then ask: What is the original meaning from which diverse meanings manifest?

If the problems of science are overcome by the symbolic treatment of matter, then meaning is the primordial reality, although this meaning exists in diverse forms of this world, such as tables and chairs, properties like color and shape, etc. These meanings form a class hierarchy in which the abstract meaning generates the contingent meaning. To trace the origin of all meaning, we must go to the root of this hierarchy. This root—in Vedic philosophy—is God and He is the form of six original meanings. The diversity of meaning springs from these six meanings as a seed expands into a tree.

God's role in this approach to the divine is not necessitated by our personal needs to believe in the divine. It is rather impelled by the problems of incompleteness in science, which propel us toward the study of the material world as diverse meanings. Once we have revised our understanding about matter, then the existence of God is indeed a scientific question, as Dawkins asserts. It, however, requires a fundamental revision to materialism; matter is no longer physical properties but diverse kinds of meanings. This revision in science must occur before God can be a scientific question.

God's Existence and Semantic Science

If theories of matter are incomplete without incorporating meaning, then the origin of the universe is also incomplete without the origin of meaning. A universe that is comprised only of physical properties clearly has no role for God. But a universe comprised only of such properties is also incomplete, indeterministic, and uncertain.

The question of the existence of God is therefore tied to the question of whether the uncertainty, indeterminism, and incompleteness of science are *ontological* features of reality or only *epistemic* problems of the current scientific theories describing this reality. In other words, is nature indeterministic and our theories simply report this indeterminism? Or is nature causally complete but our theories are not able to completely capture the nature of that causality? Even if both alternatives are *prima facie* equally likely from the standpoint of modern science, it is not difficult to see that if nature is causally complete, and we can build theories of nature that are causally complete, then these theories will make more predictions than the causally incomplete theories. A theory that makes more predictions is obviously a better theory than the one that leaves some facts unpredicted thereby leading to indeterminism. Furthermore, a theory which depicts nature as being causally complete is better than the one that depicts it as being incomplete.

The question about the existence of God is therefore indeed a scientific question. But it is also a question that goes to the root of the problems of uncertainty, indeterminism, and incompleteness in science. Science stumbles on these problems because scientific theories describe symbols of meanings as objects without meanings. Meanings cannot be constructed from an aggregation of material objects although material objects can be constructed from meanings. The science of meaning will therefore include the predictions of current science but go beyond them. Once the material objects are produced from meanings, we must now ask: From where are the meanings produced? We saw earlier how the creation of meaning can be understood as being produced from an origin of all meaning.

All meaning in the material world exists as distinctions or oppositions. There are individual observers who choose one side of the distinction. However, the opposition between these conflicting sides is reconciled in a more abstract concept. For example, the conflict between white and black is reconciled in the concept of color. So, to understand the diversity, and yet grasp its origin from a unity, we must rise up the conceptual hierarchy. In this case, this rising involves going beyond the distinctions and seeking their origin.

There can be choices that choose one side of the distinction, and there must be choices that produce both sides of the distinction. The person observing the lower parts of this hierarchy will see the oppositions and choose one of them. But the person higher in the hierarchy will find greater unity and lesser oppositions. At the root of this hierarchy, all conflicts, oppositions, and contradictions will be reconciled. In Vedic philosophy, God's consciousness is different from our consciousness, because the former constitutes the unity underlying the diversity. His consciousness is the root in which all contradictions, oppositions, and distinctions are reconciled.

The existence of God thus becomes necessary when nature is symbols rather than objects. A universe without God is a universe without meanings. The existence of God—as someone who makes a difference in the universe—is, therefore, a scientific question. Very specifically, this implies that nature is comprised of symbols rather than objects. If we describe symbols as objects, we are describing them incompletely. This incompleteness pervades current science, and it is thus important to understand its wider implications.

A Quick Survey of Incompleteness

While an exhaustive discussion of scientific problems cannot be done in the limited space here, I will briefly try to describe them through examples. I will take one example in mathematics and another one in physics. The reader is referred to my other work (*Gödel's Mistake* and *Quantum Meaning*) for an in-depth discussion.

Let's begin with mathematics. The problem of mathematics is that numbers can be described in three different ways—as things, concepts, and names—but mathematics cannot deal with these distinctions without incorporating an explicit role for meanings. Let's illustrate this problem with the following three sentences:

- Nobody has six letters
- Nobody is perfect
- I am nobody

In the first statement, the word 'nobody' is a *thing* or a sequence of six letters. In the second statement, the word 'nobody' is a *name* that refers to people. In the third statement, 'nobody' represents the *concept* of insignificance. Now, if we used these words interchangeably, we can create interesting conclusions such as the following:

- Nobody is perfect. I am nobody. Therefore, I am perfect.
- Nobody is perfect. Nobody has six letters. Therefore, perfect has six letters.

In the first case, we have arrived at an erroneous conclusion but it is not logically incorrect. In the second case, we have arrived at a logical contradiction because the word 'perfect' has seven letters and not six. It is easy to understand the source of these paradoxes. The problem is that the word 'nobody' can denote things, concepts, and names. To use language correctly, we must respect these categorical distinctions. Erroneous conclusions and logical paradoxes can arise when these distinctions are not honored. Kurt Gödel used this type of reasoning in mathematics to arrive at contradictions. The genesis of the contradiction lies in the fact that mathematics cannot distinguish between names, concepts, and things. If meanings exist in nature, then mathematics cannot describe them without logical paradoxes. This is called Gödel's Incompleteness Theorem.

Gödel's incompleteness is relevant to physical theories because in current science material objects are incapable of representing concepts and names. Every physical object in current science only describes itself rather than other objects. Similarly, physical objects only refer to themselves and not to other objects. If, therefore, physical objects are used to represent names and concepts, then such objects would be indistinguishable from things that describe themselves and only name themselves. It follows that the categorical distinction between things, names, and concepts cannot be maintained in current physical theories, and without the ability to maintain such a categorical distinction, any attempt to use objects to denote names and concepts will lead to logical contradictions. We can conclude that such physical theories—and the objects they describe—are either inconsistent or incomplete. If the theory attempts to incorporate names and concepts, then it will be inconsistent. If the theory avoids names and meanings, then it will be incomplete. Current physical theories avoid names and meanings and reduce everything to independent objects that only identify themselves and describe themselves. All such physical theories are incomplete because nature also has the ability to encode names and meanings.

Let's now turn to the problem of quantum theory in physics. I will illustrate the quantum problem with the example of an ATM. Assume that you are drawing $100 from an ATM. When you draw this money, you don't know in advance the *denominations* of the currencies you will get. You can get, for example, $100 as 1 x $50 and 5 x $10, or you may get 9 x $10 and 2 x $5, etc. You can only know that you will get a total of $100 but you don't know the denominations. Now let's further assume that each of these currency notes has the same physical size and weight, so there is no way to distinguish them physically. You need to be able to read the currency note to understand its value. Without that literacy it is just a piece of paper. In the same way, if matter is symbols of meaning, then the physical properties become inadequate to decide the symbol's meaning.

The measurement is unable to detect the symbolic meaning but can only detect the number of times an object is received. It computes probabilities of the occurrence of an event rather than the total amount of meaning—e.g. value of the cash—being received.

Quantum theory similarly tells us that when we measure an ensemble of particles, there are several ways in which we can divide the whole ensemble into parts, and each part represents the probability of a detector receiving a quantum particle. In our analogy, this corresponds to the probability of a user receiving a certain number of currency notes, without knowing their true denomination.

In addition, when you get the money from the ATM, you cannot be certain if the $50 notes will come before $10 or vice versa. The same amount of money can be delivered to you using the same denominations in many different *orders.* But this problem will follow only when we treat the events as currency denominations. The same total value can be delivered through the same parts, but in many different orders, and we cannot predict the order in advance.

These two types of indeterminism in quantum theory can be resolved if we treat quantum objects as symbols of meanings. The indeterminism of denominations will now represent a choice of vocabulary while the indeterminism of denomination order will represent the choice of a word sequence to form a sentence. The probabilities of current quantum theory would be partially irrelevant, because they will correspond to how often a certain denomination is obtained without knowing the denominational value. How frequently we get the currency notes is irrelevant to the value being delivered unless we know the denominations. We must treat the notes not as pieces of paper but as symbols of monetary value. Then we can decode the probabilities into an order which becomes an order of symbols, like a proposition it will encode a more complex meaning.

While current quantum theory cannot predict the denominations (words) and their order (sentences), these can be predicted if reality is symbolic. The same meaning can be denoted using different words and order in the words, which helps explain that we are observing the same reality. The observation, however, pertains only to the *expression* of reality and not to reality itself. That is, reality exists as value rather than as currency notes which express this value. The same meaning can be expressed through different sentences which involve different words and word sequences. It is only through the recognition that meanings are logically prior to sentences can the quantum problem be satisfactorily solved.

Implications of Incompleteness

The above description of incompleteness in mathematics and physics is by no means an exhaustive account of all the problems in science; the reader is referred to my other books for a more detailed discussion. Since the topics involved more technicalities, I have tried to paraphrase them through intuitive and simple examples here. This is only indicative of the kind of approach needed to address the problems of indeterminism and incompleteness within science.

One of the key concepts arising from an analysis of the problems of incompleteness is a conception of reality in which the whole is more real than the parts and the parts are created by dividing the whole. When parts are defined in relation to the whole, a new way of understanding the parts is needed because traditionally science has treated the parts independently of each other and the whole is simply seen as an aggregation of the independent parts. But when the wholes are prior to the parts, the parts acquire meanings in addition to a physical existence. For instance, a plank of wood becomes a leg in relation to the chair, acquiring a function. To describe these properties, the mathematical theories must also be different. Current mathematical and physical theories assume independent objects and object collections only aggregate these independent parts. A semantic description of reality, however, needs a mathematical theory that defines wholes logically prior to the part definition.

When the whole is logically prior to the parts, then the whole must exist as an abstract meaning. The fact that this meaning is encoded as a physical object is irrelevant. What is relevant is that it encodes a different meaning. It follows that a chair exists in some form before it is manifested as a collection of wooden planks, in a way like the meaning exists in some form in the mind before it is manifest as a sentence. We are intuitively acquainted with this idea. For instance, before the chair is produced, a *design* of the chair exists in the mind of the carpenter. The design is subsequently converted into the chair. The parts of the chair become legs, back, and seat because they are defined in relation to the whole and not independently. We must now say that the *idea* of the chair is logically prior to the chair and the chair is produced from that *idea*. Now, we cannot insist that the chair is only an epiphenomenon of the parts because the whole is logically prior to the parts. Similarly, in the previous example, the $100 is real even prior to the denominations in which that money is delivered at the ATM. The same money can be divided into parts in many ways, and the only way we can understand this division is if the $100 is viewed as being logically prior to the denominations.

Current theories of nature treat aggregations of atoms and molecules as epiphenomena of the sub-atomic particles which are logically prior. If the molecules are aggregated randomly, the meanings, structure, and function are byproducts of randomness. The problem of meaning in nature, however, makes the whole logically prior and equally (if not more) real than the parts. Now, meanings are not epiphenomena; they are more fundamental than the objects.

Current science claims meanings to be epiphenomena of material aggregation. This claim is false because meanings involve abstraction, contextuality, and references, which cannot be encoded into material objects. Meanings cannot be epiphenomena of material aggregations and attempts to encode meanings in independent objects will lead to logical contradictions, as Gödel's incompleteness proves. Of course, if nature does indeed encode meanings which we describe as physical objects, then the additional contextual, referential, and abstraction properties in these symbols of meaning cannot be captured by a purely physicalist account of nature resulting in the incompleteness and indeterminism of such physical theories. This is indeed the reality of all current physical theories which are unable to completely explain the properties of the aggregations themselves. The only viable solution to these problems is to recognize that meanings are logically prior to objects and they, in turn, create objects.

The question of the origin of the universe is now a question about the origin of meanings. If meanings were epiphenomena of matter, then matter would be the primary reality and meanings would be the byproducts of a material aggregation. However, problems in physics show that we cannot completely describe an aggregation of independent parts. Problems in mathematics show that we cannot provide a mathematical theory of meaning if meanings arise from objects. We can now attribute the incompleteness of science to the fact that they are trying to describe symbols but formulating that description in terms of physically independent objects.

A newer theory of matter that describes objects as symbols is now needed. In this theory, independent objects do not aggregate to create meanings. Rather, meanings divide from abstract to contingent to create objects. The incompleteness of current mathematics and physics can be addressed if meanings are logically prior to objects and objects are produced as epiphenomena of meanings.

The Question of Origins

The problem of meaning changes the questions of origins because we cannot seek the origin of matter without the origin of meaning. If meanings create objects, then the origin of objects can be solved by admitting a natural role for meanings. However, the problem of origins will not be solved only by acknowledging such a role. We must also seek the origin of all *ideas*. In fact, ideas are logically prior to things and things are produced from ideas. If the universe was purely a product of material processes, then there could not be meanings in nature, nor any ideas, descriptions, and names by which one thing can call out, describe or represent another thing. The fact that meanings exist in nature, and they cannot be reduced to aggregations of things implies that things themselves have to be described in a new way compatible with the existence of meanings.

Now, we must ask: What is the origin of all meanings, which in turn produce objects? If nature is without meaning, then material objects suffice to describe nature. However, if nature encodes meanings, then the meanings are logically prior to matter. Before we can speak about the origin of all objects, we must speak about the origin of all meanings. This dramatically changes the issue of origins, from the study of the origin of objects to that of the origin of meanings.

Origins and God

We must now say that meanings originate in the ability in consciousness to perceive and create meanings. The meaning knowing and creating faculty of the soul is called *chit* in Vedic philosophy. From this *chit* emanate the knowledge of senses and action, which are controlled by the mind. The senses of knowledge, along with the mind, perceive meanings. And the senses of action, along with the mind, create meanings. But the senses and the mind are material; they are like still water bodies in which meaning is a wave. These waves are called *vritti* or modifications. The first aphorism in Patanjali's Yoga Sutra states that the purpose of yoga is to stop the *vritti* or modifications of the *chitta* or the *chit* capacity of the soul. When the *chit* has been calmed in this way, the soul is able to withdraw its focus from the material activity and is able to see the native spiritual potency or ability to produce and consume meanings. Therefore, the *chit* aspect of the soul is considered the origin of all meanings.

These meanings, as already noted, come in six varieties—namely, knowledge, beauty, fame, power, wealth, and renunciation. Each of these categories also produces opposite types of meanings. Each soul can create a subset of all possible meanings, and these meanings are not always consistent. Indeed, meanings are created through distinctions, such as black-white, hot-cold, bitter-sweet, etc. Something cannot be black and white simultaneously; it cannot be hot and cold or bitter and sweet at once. Accordingly, the consciousness must choose to create or consume one side of the distinction. Also, as we discussed earlier, in the primordial state of matter and consciousness, all these meanings are reconciled in an inactive state. So, the origin of these meanings reconciles the opposites, and since this origin is God, the opposites are reconciled in His person.

The creation of the oppositions requires a different kind of consciousness in which the opposites can be reconciled. Our consciousness can choose only one side of a distinction, but not opposites simultaneously. That necessity implies the need for a Supreme Soul. In Vedic philosophy, all conscious beings are qualitatively similar because they can experience one side of distinctions such as hot-cold, black-white, bitter-sweet, etc. However, they are quantitatively different in the number of alternatives they can choose simultaneously. God, in Vedic philosophy, is *defined* as the consciousness which can choose all alternatives at once, including mutually opposed alternatives. He can thus create all possible meanings simultaneously.

A meaningful material universe is also a universe of opposites because meanings themselves are defined through distinctions. In a semantic space, this means that the soul is *localized* to a region of differentiated space whose locations are diverse meanings. To know something, one must be at a particular place representing that meaning. As one 'expands' their consciousness, they can become aware of more than one thing at a time. However, the soul is inherently limited in its ability to expand. Thus, it can cover multiple alternatives but not all the possible alternatives. This is where God becomes a theoretical necessity because no individual soul can know or create all the possible distinctions and varieties in the world.

Semantics necessitates the existence of consciousness, but it only implies the existence of some part of the entire universe of all contradictory meanings. For a universe of many contradictory meanings to exist simultaneously, a supreme consciousness is logically necessary. This supreme consciousness is God. God, in Vedic philosophy, is said to be capable of all contradictory choices at once. While individual sides of a distinction are relative truths of ordinary living beings, God as the choice of all possible alternatives at once is the Absolute Truth. No individual soul can create these opposites simultaneously. God is therefore the creator of all the oppositions because He can choose them at once through His infinite choice.

The Role of God in Science

The atheistic challenge to the existence of God is based on a rather premature and incomplete understanding of material nature. When nature is understood as a representation of meaning (in order to solve paradoxes and address issues of completeness), then science will require the hypothesis of a consciousness that can inject meanings in matter and thereby produce material objects. At that point, we will realize that no individual being is capable of creating all possible meanings, even though we are capable of producing different sides of the opposites. Since meanings are defined by opposites, one side of the meaning cannot exist by itself. Since no ordinary consciousness can create these opposites, only a consciousness capable of thinking the opposites simultaneously can create them.

The existence of God follows from the problems that arise in the creation of meanings. Current science is three steps removed from that problem. First, current science does not understand the role meanings play in matter. Second, once this problem is solved, science would still not understand the origins of meanings and would require the postulate of consciousness. Third, even when we postulate conscious choices, we still cannot explain the creation of opposites, because choice implies selection of only one side. The existence of God becomes a scientific question when we begin to speak about the origin of a semantic universe containing many opposites.

In Vedic philosophy, God is the originator of the *language* of opposites. He creates all possible distinctions so that a living being can choose some logically consistent subset of these possibilities. All living beings—including God—can *understand* the same language of opposites, but only God can create all the opposites at once.

The existence of God, therefore, brings the following important difference to science: nature is comprised of semantic distinctions which become the basis of objects distinctions, and the individuality of things. This changes how we conceive theories of nature; specifically, all areas of modern science have to be revised to incorporate meanings. Current scientific challenges to the existence of God are based on physicalist theories about nature, which are in themselves incomplete so long as they don't explain the origin and creation of meaning and are bound to be inconsistent if meanings were epiphenomena of physical aggregations. If the theory based on which science challenges the existence of God is itself inconsistent or incomplete, then how can the conclusions be useful and viable?

The existence of God has scientific implications and His existence makes an empirical difference to the world. To understand this difference we need semantic theories of matter, which can overcome the incompleteness and inconsistencies in modern science. These theories will point towards the existence of consciousness which can choose and produce subsets of meanings. However, this choice and creativity itself depends on the possibility for the existence of opposites, which only God can create. The study of meaning within matter not only illuminates the nature of matter, but also provides a definition of the soul and God as two different kinds of creators.

Now, we can conceive two types of choices—those that pick one side of a distinction and those that pick all the sides of the distinction simultaneously. Choices of the former type still belong in the domain of logic and laws of nature can describe the effects and consequences of choices that pick only one side of a distinction. God's choices, however, cannot be logically described because they choose the opposites simultaneously. However, God's choices must exist for a semantic universe to come into existence and for logic to operate in that universe! Thus, God cannot be described logically, but His existence would be indicated by the existence of meaning and logic.

The atheism in current science is not a problem for religion but for a theory of mind. Science cannot explain the origin of meanings by supposing that meanings are epiphenomena of objects. Once problems of meaning within science have been fixed, the natural question would not be about the origin of matter but about the origin of meanings. God as the originator of meanings becomes relevant in science when science itself will have transformed to address problems of meaning. The existence of God can therefore be scientifically discussed, but only when science has been suitably transformed..

7

Space-Time and God

Three Notions of God

In the previous article, I described how individual living beings are capable of choosing the same ideas as God but are incapable of choosing them all at once. It is a fact about the current universe that distinctions in nature are expressed through locations in space. For instance, if an object is at a different location in semantic space, then it is a distinct type of object. Distinctness between locations therefore also represents a distinction between meanings. The inability to choose multiple ideas at the same time is thus indicated by the fact that we cannot be simultaneously at many locations in space.

The ability in God to choose all the possible alternatives at once implies one of the following three possibilities about the nature of God. First, that God could be outside space because if He is outside space, then He is not constrained by the limits of being at one specific location in space and He can thus choose all alternatives simultaneously. Second, God could be simultaneously present at all locations in space, because if He is present at all locations, then again He can choose every possible event in nature simultaneously. Third, God could be at the origin of space, because at the origin of a semantic space all contradictory semantic oppositions are reconciled similar to how the origin in a geometrical space can be denoted by the number 0 which represents the sum of positive and negative numbers[5].

The idea that the universe is semantic leads to three other ideas.

---

5   While I have described this idea casually here, the notion that zero is not just a number, but the combination of all possible (positive and negative) numbers is a different approach to numbers that is out of scope here.

First, it tells us that the cause of the universe must be some conscious-ness because otherwise nature would be a collection of things, not a collection of meanings. Second, it tells us that a consciousness that can choose only one thing at a time could not create the universe, because meanings are constructed from distinctions and they require oppo-sites to exist at the same time. Third, it provides a definition of the nature of the supreme consciousness in terms of our ordinary notions of choice and space locations.

There are thus three possible notions about God, based on seman-tics. First, there can be an idea of God who is nowhere in space. Sec-ond, there can be an idea of God who is everywhere in space. Third, there can be a notion of God who is the origin of space. Which of these three notions about God should be true and real?

The Three Gods of Vedic Philosophy

Vedic philosophy claims that all these three notions are real. That is, God is nowhere, He is everywhere and He is the origin of space. These three notions about a supreme consciousness are however repre-sented by three different *forms* or personalities of God. These forms are said to have different names and functions as follows:

Kāraṇodakaśāyī Viṣṇu is nowhere
Kṣīrodakaśāyī Viṣṇu is everywhere
Garbhodakaśāyi Viṣṇu is the origin of space

To understand these three notions of God, we can consider the nature of the soul, which involves three properties called *sat, chit,* and *ananda*. The term *sat* represents relations to things. We also call this the consciousness of the living entity by which it establishes a rela-tion to a different part of the observed world. The term *chit* represents cognition and action; it constitutes the material body and mind of the soul. It includes all the concepts of knowledge (such as seeing, tasting, touching, smelling, and hearing) and the concepts of action (such as holding, pushing, walking, procreation, etc.). Finally, the term *ananda* represents the pleasure of the living entity. It is comprised of latent desires which produce pleasures when they are fulfilled and unhappiness when they unfulfilled. With these three ideas, we can understand the three forms of *Viṣṇu* as each form manifests a different aspect of the soul.

The form of God called *Kāraṇodakaśāyī Viṣṇu* is outside the universes. He creates *Pradhāna* which is the state of material energy in which all the three modes of nature are in an indistinguishable state. Into this *Pradhāna, Kāraṇodakaśāyī Viṣṇu* injects the soul through His glance. This glance should be understood as His consciousness, and when the soul is injected into matter, the soul acquires an identity different from the other souls. We can say that the soul becomes aware of the existence of other souls and is able to see his distinction from the other souls. This state is considered materially contaminated relative to the state called *Brahman* where the soul doesn't have an individual identity or individuality. In the *Brahman* state, the consciousness of each soul is directed inward rather than outward. That is, the soul is aware of its own existence, but isn't aware of the existence of the other souls. The *Pradhāna* is therefore called the 'external' energy of God because it directs the consciousness of the soul outwardly. Once consciousness is directed outwardly, the subsequent stages of matter emerge from *Pradhāna.* These are called *prakriti, mahattattva, ahamkara,* and the five gross elements. These elements (beginning with *mahattattva*) constitute the seven 'coverings' of the universe. They are all primordial elements of nature.

Once the primordial material elements and the awareness of individual soul about the other souls have been created, then the cosmic manifestation is produced by a form of God called *Garbhodakaśāyi Viṣṇu*. He produces the universe of all possibilities, which includes the space that constitutes the different planetary systems, which are the subject of Vedic cosmology. This cosmology pertains to the creation within a single universe. We might note that at this stage of creation, there are no living bodies, humans, animals, or demigods. The universe is described in the Vedic texts as being produced as a lotus from the navel of *Garbhodakaśāyi Viṣṇu.* At the summit of this lotus sits the first created being called *Brahma* who then produces all the species of life including, aquatics, plants, animals, and humans. The universe of fourteen planetary systems is said to rest vertically inside the stem of the lotus and expands horizontally from that stem. The expansion of the stem creates the universal space. This space corresponds to the *chit* of the soul as it comprises all the possibilities of concepts and actions, from which *Brahma* fashions the bodies and minds of the various species. Hence, we can say that *Garbhodakaśāyī Viṣṇu* creates the ingredients from which the various types of bodies and minds are produced by *Brahma*.

As the soul gets embodied, it develops a personality of desires, likes and dislikes, which then create pleasure and pain. The material body and mind are not the individuality of the soul, because the soul can leave one body or mind and enter another. Through this transmigration, the personality of the soul is carried forward. As the personality evolves in a given life, the next life is determined by the personality developed during the previous lifetimes. For instance, if a person develops the personality of a dog—e.g. by serving a master, fighting with others over territorial integrity, and being possessive about the place where it lives—then he enters a dog's body.

This personality constitutes an individual whereas the body and mind are created from universal elements. Our individual material bodies and minds are combinations of the universal and the individual. Due to the universals, we can describe the body in terms of universal properties like shape, size, color, parts of the body such as hands, legs, etc., which are concepts found all over the universe. However, each body is also an instantiation of the universal. For instance, there is the universal concept of a dog, and then an individual dog. The individual dog combines the individual and the universal; the universals allow us to describe the dog using concepts, while the individuality differentiates one dog instance from another.

The third form of God in each universe is called *Kṣīrodakaśāyī Viṣṇu* Who constitutes the individual. He is present with each individual soul and is also present in each individual atom. He is the original representation of individuality from which many individual instances are created. We can also call *Kṣīrodakaśāyī Viṣṇu* the principle of instantiation of the universals into individuals by which a universal idea is converted into many instances of the universal.

Thus, we can say that *Kāraṇodakaśāyī Viṣṇu* is the transcendent form of God, Who is outside the universe. *Garbhodakaśāyī Viṣṇu* is the origin of the material universe (and there are many universes in Vedic cosmology, each of which has one *Garbhodakaśāyi Viṣṇu*). Finally, *Kṣīrodakaśāyī Viṣṇu* is the immanent form of God. Thus, through these forms, God is transcendent, immanent, and the origin. Each of the three aspects of God, however, produces a possibility. Thus, consciousness is a possibility of interacting with different individuals, matter is the possibility of being converted into an individual, and the individuals are possibilities of desires. Once these possibilities have been created, the Vedas describe steps by which they are experienced under the influence of individual choices, *karma,* and time.

The Role of Causal Time

Time is that agent that converts possibilities into reality. However, this reality is not the reality of a specific individual—i.e. their individual conscious experiences. In Vedic philosophy, time determines the events in the universe (i.e. *what* will happen in the universe) before individual observers choose them (i.e. *who* will do it). While the three forms of God define all the possibilities in the universe, two things are still undetermined: the *order* in which these possibilities will be realized at the cosmic level and the specific consciousness that will experience a specific possibility at any given time. Of course, if each consciousness chooses its own possibilities, it will also determine the cosmic possibilities although it would mean that the evolution of the cosmos depends on the choices of the individuals. In Vedic philosophy, the evolution of the cosmos is determined by time and not by individual choices. Time selects a subset of all the possibilities and defines the temporal evolution of the universe.

The domain of all possibilities is space. This space is converted into real events by time. This time, however, is not the time of the individual observer, but the time of the universe as a whole. In short, this time determines the events in the universe as a whole.

Time determines what happens in the universe, not who does it. Time is also said to be a form of consciousness, which chooses from the possibilities to create a reality. Time is hence identified with a supreme person called *Śiva* or *Saṅkarṣaṇa* in Vedic philosophy. He is said to be the controller of the universe because He determines which parts of the possibilities are converted into reality by choosing the parts and ordering them as realities within time.

The individual living beings too have choices by which they can pick from amongst the possibilities available at any time, but they cannot define the possibilities that exist outside time or the possibilities at any given time. The ability in the individual living being to choose is thus subject to conditions of space and time, and the living being is said to be bound by these material conditions. What a living being can choose from the available possibilities is further constrained by that living being's *karma*, which I shall discuss later.

Note how the description of space, time, and matter differ so radically in Vedic philosophy and modern science. In science, the universal space and time always exist and a random fluctuation in space and time produces independent objects. In Vedic philosophy all objects are symbols of meaning and they are created as distinctions. The origin of the distinctions lies in the three basic modes of nature. Time then selects a subset of these types to create the individual living being who enjoys or suffers in the cosmos. At each step of this creation, there is a central role for consciousness and choice. In fact, space and time are themselves products of choice.

As noted earlier, the central problem in both science and religion is the explanation of how an undivided and undifferentiated material reality becomes the diversity of the visible cosmos. In science, either the cosmos is assumed to be *a priori* differentiated, or this differentiation is supposed to be a random occurrence. In Vedic philosophy, the creation of space, time, and objects (differentiation) and the evolution of the cosmos are successive choices. These are not necessarily *our* choices, but they are choices nevertheless.

Relative and Absolute Space-Time

Since the advent of relativity in physics, it has widely been believed that the origin of space and time is relative to each individual observer in the universe and we cannot define an absolute space and time coordinate frame because there is no universal observer. In Vedic philosophy, there is an absolute space-time because there are two primary observers who respectively represent the origin of space and of time. However, the notion of an absolute space-time is a semantic and not a physical notion. That is, the space in the universe is a space in which each location represents a different type. Similarly, the time in the universe is a time in which each instance is a different type. We briefly discussed earlier how a semantic space and time are hierarchical rather than linear. New theories of space and time are needed to understand matter semantically.

In a semantic universe, reality is symbols of ideas. But it is produced from possibilities, which are ideas as well. The universe of all possibilities can be known at once, but this knowledge is different from experience. The forms of God which create possibilities are thus knowers of material reality but not experiencers of that reality. They are in contact with material nature, but this contact is not enjoying or suffering the content produced by nature. The forms of *Viṣṇu*, therefore, know everything in the universe, but they don't experience it as we do. This means that despite knowing the universe, they are not enjoying or suffering from that experience. Their knowledge is intellectual awareness of our experience but not first-hand contact with it. *Śiva*, on the other hand, is closer to experience (as compared to the three *Viṣṇu* forms) because He actualizes the possibilities into the universal reality. While *Viṣṇu* forms know the possibilities, *Śiva* knows and creates the material reality. However, even He is not the individual experience of a specific living being, and even though He knows reality, He does not experience it like us. *Śiva's* experience is 'smaller' than the knowledge of all the possibilities in *Viṣṇu* because the reality is a subset of possibilities. But *Śiva's* experience is 'bigger' than the experiences of individual beings because *Śiva* chooses the cosmic reality from which we only choose our individual experiences. *Śiva's* consciousness is therefore said to lie in between that of *Viṣṇu* and other individual living beings.

I have discussed in *Gödel's Mistake* and *Quantum Meaning* how a semantic space-time must be an absolute space-time because in a semantic space-time the names equal to meanings. If we invert the space-time, we would not just invert names (the coordinate frame numbers) but also their meanings. It would mean that if a location denotes the meaning 'hot' and a coordinate frame inversion maps that location into the name 'cold,' then the objects at that location would also have to become cold. If all arbitrary coordinate transforms were allowed in a semantic space-time, then the universe would not have any fixed properties; each observer could view the world in arbitrary ways, describing the same world through different words. It would now be impossible to communicate the results of observations since in a typed universe different words (such as hot and cold) would be used to describe the same objects. This undesirable and impractical scenario is avoided if there is an absolute space-time. A detailed discussion of this problem is out of scope here, hence the interested reader is referred to the above books.

The interesting takeaway from this discussion is that when science evolves to study meanings, it will not only restore the idea that there are individual consciousness and supreme consciousness but it will also define the nature of the supreme consciousness based on the facts about material space and time in the cosmos. The ideas of the soul and God, therefore, follow from a revision to the scientific notions about matter, space, and time, which in turn are outcomes of the attempts to fix incompleteness in current theories. The scientific claim that the soul and God are unnecessary holds true only if science is consistent and complete, which is currently not the case.

Science and Personalism

Philosophies of impersonalism and voidism claim that variety in the universe arises from something formless. In the personalist school, all variety emanates from a person. The personalist school draws a fundamental distinction between individual consciousness as one that can only be at one location and time, and God's consciousness, which can be outside space, at the origin of space, at all locations in space, and as the collection of all manifest realities in time. To assume that individual living beings can be at all space and time at once is simply to presume something that can never be a fact.

God and the living being are different because God is capable of creating space and time, and we are capable only of *being* at a specific location and instance within that space and time. Voidism does not even postulate consciousness and it cannot, therefore, explain the origin of meanings. Impersonalism does postulate consciousness but does not distinguish between individual and supreme consciousness and it cannot thus solve the paradox of how consciousness creates meanings. Indeed, impersonalism assumes that our consciousness can be simultaneously outside and inside the universe, that it can be everywhere and everywhen, which is never a fact. The twin problems of creating all the meaning distinctions and the need for some consciousness to be outside, inside, everywhere, and everywhen requires a clear distinction between two types of consciousness—ours and God's. Personalism is therefore two main ideas: (1) that there is consciousness, which can create meanings, and (2) that individual and supreme consciousness are different.

This distinction is described at great lengths in Vedic texts, in what is also called the *Vaishnava* school of philosophy. The four forms of God described above are said to be the co-creators of material nature, and they are also called *Vasudeva* (*Kāraṇodakaśāyī Viṣṇu*), *Saṅkarṣaṇa* (*Śiva*), *Pradyumna* (*Garbhodakaśāyi Viṣṇu*), and *Aniruddha* (*Kṣīrodakaśāyī Viṣṇu*). Together these four forms of God are said to constitute the *chatur-vyūha* or the circle of four. This ancient and somewhat esoteric philosophy about the nature of God can be understood from a semantic study of material nature.

The key point is that the nature of God can be understood in a semantic universe from the need to postulate an absolute notion of space and time. In current science, every observer can potentially be at the center of the universe, by forming his or her own frame of reference which is as good as any other frame of reference. In a semantic universe, a specific type of consciousness—different from our consciousness—must be at the center or origin of the universe. The nature of the semantic universe also indicates the properties of the universal consciousness that lies at the center of the universe.

To those who believe that God is always going to be outside science, I can say that God will always be outside current science, but God's existence *can* be understood from a semantic science.

8

Are the Vedas Polytheistic?

The Many Forms of God

The problem with the description of the four forms of God in the previous essay is that it seems to suggest the Vedas are polytheistic. Vedic texts are replete with descriptions of many forms of God. Some critics of Vedic philosophy deride its descriptions by appealing to monotheism, especially as it appears in Abrahamic religions.

However, the notion that Vedic philosophy is polytheistic arises from a superficial reading. In Vedic philosophy, there is indeed one God—Who is also a person—although He divides Himself into many parts to create other forms that perform different functions. Since these forms are part of the original form, they are in some sense 'smaller' than the original form. For instance, in the previous essay we noted how the experience of the universe is smaller than the knowledge of all the possibilities in the universe, which is smaller than the combination of all the possibilities, which is smaller than the three modes of nature, and so forth. Each form of God represents a part of the total awareness, which gets successively smaller and smaller as it gets closer and closer to the awareness of matter.

Each form of God is therefore a subset of the awareness of the original form of God. All the forms are different subsets of awareness, which select from the larger awareness. The various forms of God are created by God Himself choosing to become aware of some part of His existence. These forms are called 'expansions' and They arise when God wants to know Himself. By choosing to be aware of a different part of His existence, a new form of God is created. The Vedas state that God divides and expands Himself, so the expansions are not indications of polytheism but an indication of how great the original form of God is that there are infinitely many types of focus areas for Him, which constitute aspects of His consciousness.

The standard problem for any creationist is how variety appears from a singularity. Of course, even the materialist has this problem. In the Big Bang explanation, for instance, the singularity at the beginning of the universe is an infinite concentration of energy which cannot be mathematically described due to the infinities. Every theory of origins begins in that one thing from which diversity is explained. The problem is that if there is only one thing prior to the creation of diversity, then how does this singular thing lead to the observed diversity? What makes the single become multiple? If the single is not always a single but is somehow divided by an external agency, then there must be originally at least two things rather than one. But, now, we need to ask how the two things came into existence and if there was a single thing that existed prior to these two things, thus leading to an infinite regress of original causes.

In Vedic philosophy, God is a single cause of the universe. The diversity of the creation is produced when God *divides* Himself through His choices. God is said to have three aspects—*sat* (choice), *chit* (cognition) and *ananda* (pleasure). The cognition of God is the form of six primordial *ideas* which is then expanded by the application of His choices—that are various relations of consciousness between Himself, that constitute focus on different parts of His person, thereby creating many forms of God. These choices are simply 'attention' to different parts of His person. By applying His choices to His existence, God becomes conscious of His existence and this act of being self-conscious represents God's intent to know His self. The self-knowledge also expands the primordial idea of God into many forms, which in turn expand in many ways to create the universe. The universe is therefore an outcome of God's intent to know His self, and every part of the universe is produced from God. These parts are not identical to the whole that preceded the parts.

The identity of these parts is defined only in relation to the whole. The correct way to understand the diversity is to recognize that the whole is divided into parts to create diversity from singularity. For instance, the four forms of God described in the previous article are said to be the parts of a part of a part of the whole. The fact that there are many parts does not imply that there isn't a preceding whole. In fact, the parts cannot be defined and understood without their relation to the whole. The Vedic polytheism is therefore only an apparent problem and a proper understanding of Vedic philosophy requires us to see the whole-part relationship[6].

Spiritual Functionalism

Just as an idea is divided to create individual things, similarly, God as the complete idea divides into parts to create many forms of God. Each such form of God is an increasingly smaller *part* of the whole. While we can say that the whole is each of the parts, we cannot say that the parts are the whole. In that sense, knowing the whole includes the knowledge of all the parts, but not vice versa.

Recall from the previous article that God's consciousness is supreme in the sense that He can choose diverse alternatives at once. God as the original idea is, therefore, the sum of all diversity; diversity is created when God divides Himself. All this diversity exists "inside" God because it is a smaller part of the entire whole.

The different forms of God are different parts of God. They are capable of making multiple choices at once, but as the parts become smaller and smaller, the extent of this choice reduces gradually. For example, *Kṣīrodakaśāyī Viṣṇu* can know all the possibilities at once.

6   The idea that the universe is produced from God's intent to know His being is similar in some ways to Hegel's idea that being attempts to think itself and the universe is produced from 'thought thinking thought'. The primary difference between Hegel and Vedic philosophy is that Hegel believed that absolute being is unthinkable so when that being thinks itself nothingness is produced. This nothingness then conflicts with the being creating a process of conflict and struggle between the opposites. In Vedic philosophy, when being thinks itself, the being is divided into many parts because the act of thinking involves choices which add information to the primordial idea. Through thought God concretizes a primordial idea of Godness into many individual manifestations of this primordial idea, quite like we might explain the idea of a table by concretizing it into a 'study table' and a 'dining table'. The idea of being is so primordial that it can be concretized in infinite ways, creating infinite amount of variety and differentiated objects in the universe.

Śiva however only experiences a subset of these possibilities. The scope of *Śiva's* experience is, therefore, smaller than the knowledge in *Kṣīrodakaśāyī Viṣṇu*. Similarly, while *Śiva* can experience the entire universe at once, the individual living beings can only experience much smaller subsets of this experience. The scope of a living being's conscious experience is therefore significantly reduced as compared to the experience produced in *Śiva's* consciousness.

In the material creation, higher forms of God are further removed from our experience. While the individual being experiences parts of reality at one time, *Śiva* experiences the whole universe at any time. *Śiva's* experience is the definition of all the roles in the universe at any time, without specifying the actors in those roles. *Kṣīrodakaśāyī Viṣṇu* further knows the entire diversified set of possibilities in nature, only a subset of which is actualized in *Śiva's* experience at any time. *Garbhodakaśāyi Viṣṇu* knows the summarization or combination of all possible diversities, so His knowledge is even more abstract than the knowledge in *Kṣīrodakaśāyī Viṣṇu*. Finally, *Kāraṇodakaśāyī Viṣṇu* knows the types from which any diversity can be created, so His knowledge is even more abstract and primordial than the knowledge within *Garbhodakaśāyi Viṣṇu*.

Vedic texts provide a detailed theory about the different forms of God and how they are produced from higher forms of God. Since a complete description of the various forms of God is out of scope here, the curious reader is referred to spiritually-focused texts, such as *Śrimad Bhāgavatām* and *Viṣṇu Purāṇa* for further details. I have only tried to capture a summary of the ideas to illustrate that the apparent polytheism in Vedic philosophy does not actually contradict the ultimate thesis of monotheism because the many forms of God are parts of the one form and are created in the act of God's self-knowledge and experience. The diversification of God's forms follows a similar pattern as the diversification of objects from an undivided and undifferentiated reality prior to the universe.

Demigods are Not God

Vedic descriptions about God end with *Kṣīrodakaśāyī Viṣṇu*. Beginning with *Śiva*, there are many subsets of this entire set of possibilities.

Thus, while *Śiva* experiences everything manifest within the universe at any one time, the Vedas also describe the presence of demigods (called *deva*) who experience smaller subsets of the cosmic experience at once. While they cannot experience opposites at the same time, they can, however, experience semantically similar types of information across many instances or objects. For instance, while you and I can experience some wealth, we cannot claim to experience all the wealth in the world; that is said to be the experience of a demigod called *Kubera.* Similarly, while you and I can have some amount of love, we cannot claim to enjoy all the love in the universe; that is said to be enjoyed by a demigod called *Kamadeva.*

These demigods have a much broader experience than us, but their experience is a much smaller subset of the experiences in *Śiva* which is further a small subset of possibilities in *Kṣīrodakaśāyī Viṣṇu* and so forth. Relative to our experiences, the demigod's experience is much broader. But relative to God's experience, the demigod experience is a pittance. Nevertheless, for those living beings whose thinking hasn't developed sufficiently enough to understand the nature of God, the Vedas prescribe an understanding of these smaller parts of the cosmic experience. In that sense, Vedic knowledge includes not just the transcendental aspects, but also mundane aspects of our life. Thus there is *Ayurveda* (the science of health), *Gandharva-veda* (the science of music), and *Vāstu-shāstra* (the science of architecture). The Vedas also provide descriptions of rituals by which a living being can obtain increased amounts of love, money, health, music, property, and other material objects. All of these together form *apara-vidya* or inferior knowledge as compared to knowledge about God Himself which is called *para-vidya* or transcendental knowledge. While the knowledge related to health, music, wealth, and architecture is more tangible in terms of what we know today, this is not the core and ultimate purpose of Vedic philosophy.

Impersonalist Distortion of Vedic Philosophy

Many Indian philosophers who wanted to rationalize the Hindu tendency to worship many 'gods' to their Western monotheistic counterparts came up with the interesting idea that we don't actually worship the 'gods' directly but a universal being *through* the individual 'gods.' They claim that the ultimate truth is impersonal, and any notion of a personal God is illusory. In fact, such philosophers claim that the notions of God and demigods are equally illusory and that the many 'gods' of Hinduism are fictional entities serving as stepping stones to the ultimate formless conception of Absolute Truth. To reconcile the impersonal notion of reality with the personal worship of deities and demigods, the impersonalist claims that the 'devotion' to the demigods (or even to God) is actually just a stepping stone for the less developed consciousness so that the devotee can actually grasp the true nature of reality, which is a grand unified, formless existence. These approaches to religion, in which the spiritual practitioner tries to see the impersonal through the personal, not only undermine the devotee that worships the demigods but also undermine an understanding about the true personal character of the single transcendent God. They claim that devotion is intended for the less intelligent people. When these people will come to the true stage of 'knowledge' they would inevitably discard all worship.

In some cases, this philosophy is further extended to weave in the Christian concept of 'love thy neighbor' in the attempt to make religion more this-worldly rather than other-worldly (even some scientists can now sympathize with it—openly and not just as closet believers). The extension now says that if we can worship the transcendent God through many individual 'gods,' why can't we do the same by serving different human beings? If one God is manifest through many 'gods' then obviously He is also manifest through all living beings. The moral brotherhood amongst mankind in other religions then becomes a philanthropic conception of Hinduism which breeds even more confusion because the true nature of religion, which is love and worship of God, now becomes the love and worship of one's fellow being. The trouble with this idea about religion is that it is devoid of a true conception of a transcendent God. Proponents of such ideologies may be doing well-intentioned service to humanity, but their conception about religion is far from that described in the Vedic scriptures. In fact, these practices of 'religion' also do a disservice to the original Vedic religion, because they misinform their followers about the true Vedic ideologies.

Owing to these confusions, it appears that Vedic religion either portrays: (1) a multi-theistic personal conception of God in which many 'gods' can be worshiped equally well or (2) a completely impersonal notion about God in which all forms of worship are denied or regarded as temporary stepping stones. Very few people are aware that Vedic religion is in fact monotheistic. They are unaware that modern Hinduism is unlike the Vedic religion of the past. Modern Hinduism either puts all kinds of 'god' worship on the same platform or denies the existence of an ultimate personal God.

In the Vedas, the demigods are smaller than God but they have been entrusted with parts of universal administration. These demigods don't occupy their positions forever. They inhabit their administrative positions due to past good deeds but fall when their prescribed term is over. Indeed, the demigods are described as greedy and selfish; they get angry and manipulate others. They are still far superior to other living beings in terms of their abilities and the extent of their control of material nature. But they are not God. The worship of demigods is therefore openly ridiculed as *kaitava dharma* or "cheating religion" in the Vedas, because it prostitutes a higher principle of devotion to God towards mundane needs.

9

Science and Ritualism

Conceptual Causality

Polytheism is not the only perceived problem in Vedic philosophy. It is also the idea that people can worship demigods and obtain material results, that seems to violate notions about causal laws in nature as described by current science. Since ritual practices are performed through material implements, the skeptic claims that there is no causal connection between these implements and the outcome of this worship. The Vedic practices involving the chanting of *mantras* appear as mumbo-jumbo of an ancient illiterate tribe to most people who are unaware of the principles that underlie these practices. This essay will try to demystify some of these difficult concepts.

The idea that matter is symbols of information or meaning is necessary to understand the performance of Vedic rituals. The material causality in this view of nature depends not on physical properties but on meanings. As an illustration, a sound vibration can be studied as frequency, amplitude and wavelength, which are physical properties. These properties define a *tone*. However, more abstract than the tone is a *scale* within which the tone becomes a *note*. There are thus two ways in which the same sound can be described—as tones and notes. Now, if material causes are based on physical properties, then tones will completely determine the outcomes in nature. If, however, causality is based on *notes* instead of tones, then there will be some effects based on which tone represents which note.

Now someone can argue that the *scale* is also defined physically, but in Vedic philosophy it is not. The scale depends on an idea, which is then related to an emotion. For example, there are scales for

79

happiness and sadness, marriage and death, morning and afternoon, etc. Each scale is played on a different occasion suited for the mood of the occasion, the time and place, or the idea to be conveyed. Thus, even though we can physically measure the scale as some frequency, why it conveys a type of mood and idea cannot be understood in this way unless we say that the scale is derived from a mood.

Therefore, if causality is based on notes instead of tones, then the measurement of frequencies will not explain the effects produced from notes. There is some effect of the sound, but only when understood as a note can the effect be fully understood. When the sound is described as tones, the effects would not be explainable. For instance, why the music creates emotions within us would not be understood unless we say that the note is itself an idea.

It follows that a science based on physical properties will be incomplete if the causal effects in nature are based on meanings. All modern areas of science—including theories in physics, computing, and mathematics—are known to be fundamentally incomplete. This incompleteness can be related to the problems of meanings, as I have briefly illustrated through examples in earlier articles. The connection between incompleteness and meanings tells us that science must shift from describing matter as physical properties to describing meanings. Physical properties capture the nature of an object independent of other objects, whereas meanings capture the nature of an object as it relates to other objects within a context.

Vedic philosophy describes nature in terms of how our senses, mind, intelligence, ego, morality, and consciousness perceive matter. All these descriptions are semantic, and matter is the encoding of meaning as experienced by the observer, although current science describes these meanings in terms of physical properties.

Rituals and Conceptual Causality

The Vedic prescriptions of rituals are based on conceptual causality and not on physical properties. In a ritual, an ordinary material object—such as water, fire, a leaf, a flower, or food—is transformed into a symbol of some meaning by the chanting of *mantras*. The meaning here comes from the *mantra* which is a sound-symbol, and it transforms other objects too into symbols of meaning. If we only measure the physical properties of these objects—such as the weight of the water, the temperature of the fire, the size of the leaf, or the calories in the food—then we will fail to see what they represent semantically and hence the effects that these symbols are capable of. We would measure the symbols as properties of physical objects, similar to the frequencies of tones rather than the meanings of notes.

To understand the causality involved in a ritual, we have to view the objects involved in the ritual as symbols of meanings. When these symbols are 'offered' to a demigod during the ritual, the effect is not based on physical properties but rather based on their meanings. Any given object can denote several different meanings; for instance, water can be made to denote a variety of different meanings based on the *mantra* that is being chanted. The *mantra* itself is a physical object—namely, a sound vibration—but, like the tone can be understood as a note based on the scale of notes, similarly, the words in the *mantra* become symbols based on the mind.

The bodies of living beings are also conceptual matter. The demigods especially dominate concepts such as love, health, knowledge, beauty, strength, etc. When symbols of a particular concept are offered to a demigod or demigoddess, he or she is enriched by the instance of the concept just as our bodies are nourished by eating food. The demigod or demigoddess is then obliged to return the favor. This obligation is not merely a feeling of gratitude, but rather the demigod or demigoddess is bound by the law of *karma* to return the requested meaning offered to him or her by the devotee. This meaning is not an absolute property of the offered object, but a contextual property of the relation between the offering and the devotee. For instance, a small offering of a leaf or fruit by a poor devotee has the same value as an elaborate feast offered by a rich person. The effect of the offering does not depend on the physical properties of the offering (e.g., its 'size') but on its relation to the devotee. A small offering by poor person or a large offering made by a rich person has the same effect. Similarly, a small offering to a more powerful demigod has a much larger effect than the same offering to a less powerful demigod. In Vedic philosophy, demigods are much smaller than God. The Vedas therefore ultimately advise the worship of God rather than of demigods, even if you desire material goods, simply because the effects of such worship are much larger.

The demigods return the favor by furnishing instances of concepts that they were fed with. For example, the demigoddess of knowledge (called *Sarasvati* in Vedic literature) will return the favor by helping the worshipper increase their knowledge and the demigod of wealth (called *Kubera*) will return the favor by helping the worshipper increase their wealth. Note, however, once you get a large return, then the size of the subsequent offering must also be larger! These offerings thus follow the law of diminishing returns for the same offering, and the worship of demigods is not recommended because it ensnares the soul in the cycle of making larger and larger offerings to constantly increase their diminishing returns.

The Vedas advise that the living beings can worship the demigods only to fulfill their basic needs such as food, shelter, and peaceful living, and not for increasing material comforts and luxuries. If the living being is only trying to obtain the basic necessities, then a small effort and a small offering are sufficient to obtain the needs.

The symbol by which the demigod is worshipped is an abstract representation of a concept and the favor that the demigod returns is a more detailed embodiment of the same concept. Demigods are empowered living beings who know how to manipulate matter in ways that we do not. Thus, while all living beings cannot always create knowledge and wealth, they can use the abilities in the demigods to fulfill their desires. This worship is a selfish action. It is not spirituality, but rather a material transaction based on a novel kind of science in which matter is treated as symbols of meanings.

The Scientific Basis of Prayers

Every religion speaks about prayers. In Vedic philosophy, these prayers are formalized as offerings and rituals to demigods and to God. The devotees believe that prayers have an effect on their lives. Scientists claim that this could not be so, based on their theories of material nature. The devotees then claim that prayers transcend material science, although they cannot explain how that is possible. In Vedic philosophy, there are two kinds of prayers—those that are made to demigods, and to God. In both cases, overtly, the actions of the prayer are seemingly material. And yet, it is possible to understand these actions also as symbols of different kinds of meanings. When matter is viewed as symbols of meaning, then the causality is in the meaning and not in the material encoding of that meaning. Of course, this applies not just to prayers but to all material objects. It is possible to provide a scientific basis of prayers based on a different approach to the study of matter; basically, the causality in matter has to be described in terms of meanings instead of matter.

All prayers are, however, not identical. There are differences in meanings in different prayers. There are certain meanings that have *references* in the world and there are meanings which do not have a material reference. A devotee can, for instance, pray for his daily sustenance. This meaning has a material reference because the end object of that prayer is food, which exists in the material world. A devotee can also ask for God's eternal service, which does not have a material reference because in the material world nothing is eternal. Whether or not the meaning encoded in matter has a material reference, defines whether the prayer is to demigods or to God, respectively. The demigods are individuals that embody ideas, which can be referenced in the material world. God is an individual who embodies ideas that cannot be referenced within matter.

That leads to questions about which meanings are real. Let's take for instance the idea of a 'golden mountain.' It can be encoded in a symbol and we can speak about golden mountains. However, does the idea of 'golden mountain' reference something real in the world? This problem has been debated for many centuries in Western philosophy. The problem is two-fold. First, how do we understand the meaning of 'golden mountain' when no one has seen it? Plato tried to answer this question by suggesting that there is a world of ideas outside this world, which encodes every possible idea. Second, even if we accept the Platonic solution, we still have the problem of how the other world interacts with the present one. In other words, how does the idea of a 'golden mountain' appear in our minds when it exists in some other non-material world?

In Vedic philosophy, all ideas are produced from a primordial *language* called *śabda-brahmān*. The language is comprised of distinctions that we can make. For instance, we can choose between hot and cold, black and white, bitter and sweet, etc. God creates these basic distinctions and we can choose one side of the distinction. By ordering these choices, we can also create more complex ideas similar to how sentences are created by ordering words. Note how any type of idea can be encoded in matter through such order. However, the ability to produce these ideas all at once is not material because the ideas are mutually opposed, and to encode them, we would have to step outside conventional logic which is inherently consistent.

Vedic philosophy attributes the creation of all distinctions to God's consciousness and the choices between these distinctions to our consciousness. If the world is semantic, then the collection of all possible distinctions constitutes space and the order of these ideas constitutes time. God's consciousness cannot be reduced to matter because material objects have a specific location in space and time and God's consciousness spans all space and all time. Similarly, the consciousness of demigods spans multiple instances of a concept; for instance, the demigod *Varun* is aware of all instances of water, and the demigod *Agni* is aware of all instances of fire. Again, this means that their consciousness cannot be reduced to individual objects because it spans many locations and instances in space and time. Likewise, our consciousness spans the body, which is many individual locations in space-time (each location is an atomic object). While material objects can only exist in a particular location at any time, consciousness can be at many locations simultaneously. This shows a basic difference between matter and consciousness.

While we can speak about space and time, and encode these ideas in matter as words and theories, space and time are themselves not material objects. Theories about space and time *refer* to something that does not exist as an object. A theory of space and time uses these words as *names,* but they don't point to any object in space-time. It does not mean that these things don't exist. It means that they are not material. We saw earlier how some forms of God embody the ideas of space and time. We now saw how these ideas can be *named* in matter but cannot be *referenced* in matter.

Thus, ideas without a reference in matter are not necessarily meaningless. These ideas cannot be encoded in matter because they are the origin of matter. We can use *names* to call them out, and while the names can be encoded in matter, the meanings (or references) of these names do not exist in matter. If all names had to refer to objects, then we could not use 'space' and 'time' in science.

Similarly, a devotee can use names to refer to God. These are not referencing objects, but they can be encoded in matter. This is a paradoxical aspect of religion—that its object of worship is not a material object—although the object can be referenced through material objects. The paradox arises because we suppose that all material objects can encode names but refer to other material objects. This idea leads to the confusion that if a transaction involves material objects then its interaction must also be with other material objects. Semantic causality changes this view because there can be material objects that name and represent non-material objects.

The paradox of rituals and symbolism is however not limited to religion; it exists even in science as the ability to speak about space and time through symbols from within space and time. If symbols only had to refer to things inside space and time, then symbols in science could not refer to space and time. These symbols could speak about individual locations in space and time, but not about space and time as a whole. I have connected the problem of symbolism in science and religion because as we saw earlier in Vedic philosophy God's form in the material universe is connected to the nature of space and time. For instance, the three modes of nature—which are fundamental categories that create all objects—are prior to the objects and hence outside space-time. These modes cannot be spoken about from within the universe if names can only refer to objects in the universe. The scientific counterpart of this problem is the logical inability to speak about the dimensions in the universe from within the universe: If all objects exist in 3-dimensional space, then how can they describe the 3 dimensions? The fact that this is possible itself entails some interesting features about the universe. The key feature of relevance is that space and time themselves must have a form that can be encoded in the form of a word. The similarity between these forms allows us to represent the ideas of space and time through words such as 'space' and 'time' within the universe.

This possibility is very important for religion because it means that it is possible to draw a space-time picture of something that exists outside space-time. The devotees who worship such forms of God actually refer to God using a deity or form provided the form embedded in matter is like the form outside matter. A classic example of this form is the *name* being used to call God. This name must represent the meaning embodied in God's form, for it to be a true representation. Therefore, every name doesn't refer to God, but some names—which represent the form of God—are true names of God. As a name, God is present in matter. However, as the meaning or reference encoded by that name, He is also outside of matter.

Religious Imagery and Symbolism

Think of a set of all pots. Each member of the set has some unique properties; e.g., some pots may be large while others may be small. But they are all embodiments of the idea of potness, that precedes these individual pots (the idea is used to create the pots). Amongst all the various types of pots, there is a perfect pot, because it embodies all the traits of potness in perfect proportion. The perfect pot is within the set of pots, is different from the other pots, but it represents potness perfectly. There are thus three ways to think about pots: sets, instances, and the perfect instance. While the other instances embody the idea of potness, only the perfect instance captures potness uniquely. These three types of notions about the pot illustrate the problem of religious symbolism in Vedic philosophy where God is worshipped through deities (forms of God created in stone, wood, metal, etc.) and other symbols that represent the idea of God. While God is the whole inside which many individual instances of the same idea are instantiated, there is also a perfect instance of the same idea that embodies the whole perfectly.

Another commonplace example of this fact is seen in each country. The country is the collection of things which together constitute the whole. But within the country are also flags of the country that are used to represent the country collectively. There is also a head of state who is the primary instance and citizen of that country.

In a semantic world, the whole exists before the parts. Each whole denotes an idea, in relation to larger wholes. The parts in the whole are created by adding information that selects the possibilities within the whole. There is also a perfect instance of the whole within that whole. This perfect instance represents the whole, although it is a part of that whole. This makes it possible to represent the whole inside the whole and enables us to talk about the whole from within the whole. The perfect instance has a name and meaning—the name and meaning are given in relation to other instances within the whole—but it also has a reference that points to the whole. The perfect instance, therefore, symbolizes the whole within the whole, and therefore it points to the whole from inside it.

This fact about wholes, parts, and perfect instances is true for the universe. The universe consists of objects that are specific instances of space-time[7], and each object is constructed by adding information that individuates one object from another. But within this space-time there is also a perfect instance of space-time, which embodies space-time as a whole. We earlier saw how *Kāraṇodakaśāyī Viṣṇu* represents the whole space and *Garbhodakaśāyi Viṣṇu* is the perfect instance of the whole, and Who becomes the origin of the universal space. The perfect and first citizen of the universe is therefore present as a representation of the whole inside the universe. In a similar way, the Vedas describe how many different forms of God can be created as representations of God. These representations are called *deities* and they embody the whole as a part.

The instantiation of the whole within the whole is called *incarnation* where the whole appears as a part within the whole. There are many possible incarnations of God in the material world. Since matter itself is described as space-time vibrations, and the object's meaning is equated with its 'name', God's name is also an incarnation of God. God's name is an object in the material world. But this object has a meaning that perfectly represents the idea of God. The name also *refers* to the perfect instance of God outside matter.

7   Space and time, in this view, are individual entities, quite like objects, although not objects. Like the idea of a pot can be used to instantiate many individual pots, similarly, the idea of space and time can be used to instantiate many individual objects which are all part of the space-time whole.

A semantic theory of nature is needed to understand how a perfect instance of the whole is instantiated within the whole. This instantiation allows us to speak about the whole from within the whole. In a non-semantic theory, the existence of the whole within the whole will lead to a logical contradiction because we cannot distinguish between the perfect instance and the whole; both are called by the same name. But in a semantic theory, we can distinguish between the whole and the perfect instance within it and this prevents any logical contradictions. The notion therefore that God Who exists outside the universe can also be perfectly represented within the universe cannot be understood in current material science. But this idea can be understood perfectly in a semantic science.

Impersonalism results from the attempt to apply materialistic notions about space-time to interpret symbols of God, and it argues that only things in space-time have a form. To be outside space-time is to be formless. Thus, what exists outside space-time cannot be spoken of within space-time. Since forms of God represent God, who is outside space-time, these forms must be illusions. Alternately, if a form can embody formlessness, then any form can also embody it. Thus, impersonalism concludes that we are all God in the sense that our forms are also representations of the absolute formlessness that exists outside space-time. This fallacy in reasoning is a direct outcome of thinking of space-time as a physical container and not a semantic container. In a physical container, the whole cannot exist as a part in the whole, whereas in a semantic container it can.

If impersonalism is applied literally to science, it would mean that we cannot speak about space-time from within space-time. Hence, there cannot be theories of space-time, because the words 'space,' 'time,' and 'universe' would be meaningless: these words refer to the whole, and there cannot be a representation of the whole within the whole. Impersonalism will thus eliminate the existence of science. It will take away the ability to speak about the origin of space-time, within space-time. Our deepest mysteries and hardest problems would become unspeakable. If, however, it is possible to speak about space-time from within space-time, then it follows that space-time as a whole must have a form. This whole must exist as an idea that can be embodied into an object within space-time. Now, space-time is not a container of things. It is rather a container of ideas (because it can encode itself as a symbol within) and it is itself an idea (because it can be encoded as an idea within itself).

Religious Symbolism and Science

The problem of religious symbolism is not a question of faith for the believer who worships material objects. Instead, it is a deep problem about the ability to talk about the universe as a whole from within the universe. Denial of the possibility for religious symbolism will also deny the possibility for scientific theories about the origin of the universe. The problem of symbolism in religion is also not a unique fact about religion but similar to the problem of any kind of symbolism. It requires a different view of matter and space-time than provided by current scientific theories. Indeed, a revised notion of matter and space-time will not only explain any kind of symbolism, but will also explain how we can talk about space-time as a whole from within space-time without creating a logical contradiction.

Note how in the current physical view of nature the theory of nature cannot exist within nature, for the simple reason that an object within a whole cannot represent the whole. A semantic theory of nature is therefore needed to allow the existence of a theory of space-time and of the origin of the universe within the universe.

Once we can talk about space-time from within space-time, we would acknowledge that space-time has a form, because without this form it could not be represented in space-time. Since words and theories have form, the form of the theory must indicate the form of the object it describes, and in the case of a theory of space and time, the form of the theory will describe the form of space and time. For such a theory to be true, space and time itself must have a form. Semantic notions of the universe now lead us to ask: If space consists of all the distinctions, what is the form of the combination of these distinctions? If time consists of all the possibilities, what is the form of all the possibilities? These are profound scientific questions. But in a semantic world, they are also questions about the *idea* of space and time from which other idea-like things are instantiated.

As we noted earlier, the source of the universe is the soul which has three aspects—*sat* (choice), *chit* (idea), and *ananda* (pleasure). The root of the universe is a basic idea or *chit* which produces other categories. This root is divided into many shoots and leaves by information produced from *chit*. This information is represented by the three modes of nature, which create the individual conceptual locations in a semantic space with the three modes of nature constituting its dimensions. An object that has all three categories in perfect proportion can also denote the idea of space and time within space-time. The fact that space and time can be represented in space-time implies that these have a form and are not formless. Indeed, the form of space and time in Vedic philosophy is the form of the four forms of God as described in an earlier essay. Their existence represents the basic ideas of space and time, which are divided by their consciousness into infinitely many possibilities, which are selected by the effect of time into a cosmic evolution, parts of which are chosen by the individual living beings as their experiences.

The scientific questions about space-time are also the religious questions about absolute consciousness, and how it creates the universe. The symbolism in science—when it speaks about the origin of the universe—is no longer distinguishable from religious symbolism. Both symbols will have some meaning in relation to other symbols. But they also have a reference outside the universe. The Vedic theory of religious symbolism—such as the chanting of the names of God and the worship of deities and forms—will no longer be an illusion. It would rather be the most profound truth that we can speak about, understand and experience from within the universe, although the truth describes something outside the universe.

10

Do Miracles Violate Scientific Laws?

Miracles in Religion

The concept of a miracle is important in many religions, as they are the way God exercises His divine intervention in the world when He responds to prayers. Indeed, the qualification of being a saint in Christianity or other religions is to be able to effect miracles in response to prayers, allowing the worshipper to not only pray to God but also to the saints. Miracles are supposed to happen in violation of the laws of nature, which science studies. And so, the typical religionist claims that the laws of science hold sway most of the time but they could also be violated or overruled by God and His saints.

This overruling of scientific laws is understandable if we can explain the mechanism by which it is effected. Rationality demands that the changes made to the world should be rationally understood; if we cannot explain changes, then we risk becoming irrational, and the typical religionist may now acknowledge that there are certain aspects of reality that cannot be comprehended rationally.

The religious problem of explaining the role of God in material nature arises because religions claim that God is outside the universe. If God enters the universe, then scientists would claim that God would be subject to the laws of nature and His actions would be governed by material laws. Those actions could no longer be called miracles; they would have to be scientifically explained. In short, if God is outside the universe, then He cannot effect changes in the universe, because such an effect would imply something outside space-time affecting something within it. If, however, He enters the universe, then His actions must be governed by natural laws. Any disagreement on these points leads to the view that the person who is disagreeing is not a rational thinker, because rationality requires that God's influence on nature must also be rationally understood.

Miracles are another way of saying that we don't understand how things happen in the universe. Even if God can directly control nature, this control must be explained. The concepts utilized in this explanation may be different than those used in present science; but, to begin with, we need an explanation. The method by which God changes the world establishes a relation between God and matter. So, to explain miracles, we must know the relation between God and matter. However, most religions today cannot clearly explain this relation. Only Vedic philosophy can illuminate this controversy.

We saw in the previous essay that although God is outside the universe, He also appears in the universe as the perfect instance of the whole. Therefore, the first idea—that if God is outside the universe then He could not appear in the universe—is falsified in a semantic view of nature. Once God appears within the universe, then He can act just like we act and He can therefore cause changes. Now a materialist could argue that if God appears within the universe then His actions must be subject to the laws of nature as well. These laws apply to all other living beings in the universe and if the same laws apply to God as well then He too is an ordinary being. All ordinary beings have to endure the consequences of their actions. This would mean that if God acts in the universe then He too is bound by the consequences of His actions. In Vedic philosophy, the consequences of a person's action cause the cycle of birth and death and if God is under the same laws of nature then He too must undergo repeated births, deaths, old age, and suffering like the others.

This problem requires a profound understanding of the nature of laws in Vedic philosophy. The laws of nature in a semantic universe are not the laws of force in matter. They are rather the *laws of choices*. These laws allow for the existence of conscious free will and then determine the consequences of the use of that free will. To understand why God is not under the control of these laws— even when He is inside the universe—we need to comprehend the nature of choice-based laws, and their difference from the well-known force-based laws in modern science. The fact that God is free from the consequences of His actions is not a fact unique about God but about the nature of causal laws. Indeed, even ordinary living beings can be free of the consequences of their actions through a proper understanding of these laws, and freedom from the consequences of actions (and the concomitant cycle of birth and death) is the central focus of all the information the Vedas provide about natural laws.

The Role of Choice in Matter

In the Vedic view, matter is shaped by the observer's choices of what they choose to encode in matter. For instance, we all acknowledge that if a gun's trigger is pulled, a bullet will be shot. However, whether the trigger is pulled or not is a choice. Current sciences have no explanation for choice; biologists claim that the trigger pull is a neuronal impulse, which is a chemical reaction, which is based on laws of physics, which are nothing but the mathematical laws about physical forces. It would seem therefore that the person who pulls the trigger could not have done otherwise because all actions are determined by mathematical laws. If the problem of free will has to be solved, then it requires a role for choice within physics itself.

Choices also influence how matter is observed. We have seen how the meanings are objective but their *expression* into observable propositions depends on a choice; the same meaning can be expressed through different propositions. Furthermore, to decode the meanings encoded in nature, one needs an understanding of the language. While the meanings are objective, there are often gaps in understanding the context that gives specific meanings to objects. This understanding of meaning depends on the cultural, social, and linguistic conditioning in the mind, which in turn shapes our future actions, and the meanings we choose to encode in matter. The conditioning in our minds can, for instance, bias us towards perceiving the world or alter our understanding of how nature works. In a physical world, the understanding of nature does not play a role in the evolution of the universe. However, in a semantic universe, the understanding of laws determines our choices and their outcomes.

Choice and Matter in Vedic Philosophy

We have already discussed the semantic view of matter in which matter encodes information. Material things are, in this view, symbols of meaning, rather than meaningless particles. We have also discussed how meanings can be encoded in matter if wholes are divided into parts rather than aggregating meaningless parts into wholes. In fact, meaning is the relation between a part and a whole.

Once meanings have been encoded, we need a conception about changes in meanings that transform them through the use of other meanings. Let's call this *semantic causality*. We saw earlier that if nature has semantic causality then physical properties will underdetermine the causes and theories of matter based on the measurement of physical properties will be incomplete. We discussed that all areas in modern science—including physics, mathematics, and computing—are incomplete. And I showed how these problems can be overcome by incorporating a direct role for meaning in matter.

Vedic philosophy explains a new semantic causal view of nature through the notion of three categories called *soma, agni,* and *vāyu.* The term *soma* represents the desires of a person by which choices are made; we can call this intentional causality. The term *agni* represents material objects which are divided into parts through a hierarchy. The term *vāyu* represents relationships of information transfer between parts. The notion of *vāyu* loosely corresponds to the idea of force in modern science but this 'force' acts on meanings rather than on objects. Conceptual and intentional meanings are two complementary ways of describing a semantic object. For instance, we can define the meaning of a program, which is a conceptual description. This description is different from the intentional meaning which represents the problem to be solved by the program. But to the extent that a program can solve many different problems, the conceptual and the intentional descriptions are not identical.

By combining these categories phenomena are produced. I will speak about these categories together as *information*. This represents not the notions of physical information, such as that used in modern computers, but a new notion about semantic meaning.

Agni, soma, and *vāyu* together represent every system. For instance, a living body is described in terms of these three ideas, and they are called *pitta, kaphā,* and *vāta,* respectively. The Vedic theory of healing and health is based on these ideas. The choices of consciousness are effected in matter through *agni, soma,* and *vāyu.* These categories also abstract the intentional and conceptual encoding in matter as cognition in the mind. The intentional properties of an object are how it relates to an individual person. The conceptual properties are how that object relates to its parts within. And relational properties of an object are how it relates to other objects. *Soma* indicates a person, *agni* denotes the meaning or conceptual content in an object, and *vāyu* denotes the relation between objects.

The Laws of Choices

The study of choices involves two kinds of laws. First, there are laws that indicate the *effect* of choices; for instance, when the trigger is pulled, a bullet is ejected from the gun. Second, there are laws that indicate the *consequences* of choices; for instance, the trigger pull may or may not be morally correct and the actor will have to bear the good or bad consequences of his or her actions. These consequences then create the causes which then become effects. Therefore, a cause is not the product of a previous effect. It is rather produced from some consequences effected due to past actions.

Since current science only studies effects and not consequences, we need to understand how causal descriptions can incorporate consequences besides effects. If a part acts in accordance with the meaning of the whole, these actions will always produce logically consistent outcomes between the part and the whole, and between the parts themselves. Now, there is no need for *consequences* of actions. Every action results in a transformation of the parts and the whole, but the change in the parts is consistent with the change in the whole, and the change is thus not attributable to any particular part or to the whole. The parts and the whole therefore collectively evolve in a consistent manner. It follows that there is a need to understand the consequences of an action only when there is a contradiction between the part-part or whole-part relationship. For instance, the whole-part relation could indicate one meaning while the part-part relation indicates quite a different meaning.

The terms 'right' and 'wrong' are, at present, defined through the part-part relation and not through the whole-part relation. This definition of 'right' and 'wrong' represents the ordinary notion of morality, which currently prevails in most societies and religions. In this definition, the 'right' and 'wrong' are judged by what we do in relation to other parts rather than what we do in relation to the whole. While Vedic philosophy encourages 'right' actions in the above sense of part-part relations, it lays a greater emphasis on transcending these notions of morality. Every time you set out to do some good to a fellow being, you are likely to hurt other beings. Some of this hurt is legitimate but there could also be illegitimate pain. The latter leads to adverse consequences and a person may perform immoral actions in the attempt to be perfectly moral.

If the part bears a relation to the whole and acts in that relationship, no consequences (good or bad) are created. If, however, a part acts in a part-part relationship, without a full understanding of the whole-part relationship, consequences (both good and bad) will be created. In Vedic philosophy, these consequences are called *karma*, which can be either good or bad. The idea of *karma* is the variation between the meaning of the whole-part relation and the meaning of a part-part relation. There is the possibility of freedom from *karma* which is attained by acting in the whole-part relation.

Thus, while there is always an effect for every action, there may be no consequences (if actions are performed in the whole-part relation). There are, hence, morally good and bad actions, which result in good and bad consequences. But indulging in these good or bad actions is considered inferior to getting out of the cycle of actions and consequences. Aside from morally good and bad actions, therefore, there are also morally inert actions in Vedic philosophy. The living being is advised to engage in morally inert actions so that he or she is not bound to face the consequences. The living being should therefore finish reaping the consequences of past actions—whether good or bad—and if he or she is not creating new consequences, the cycle of action and consequence of that action can cease. The living being can then get out of the cycle of action and consequences, or the cycle of birth and death. The fact that some actions don't have consequences is interesting because it implies that there are some actions that would not be governed by the second type of laws mentioned above. They will obey the laws of action and effect, but the actor is not required to face the consequences of their actions.

Karma and God

The above detour into the nature of conscious causality was necessary to illustrate that God is not alone in being free from the consequences of His actions. Even other living beings can be free from the laws of nature. This freedom seems quite mysterious initially. How can the laws act sometimes, and not act at other times? What is the second-order law that determines when the law of conscious action is applied or not? And if there is such a second-order law then which third-order laws will determine whether the second-order laws are applied? This quickly leads to an infinite regress of laws. The problem can only be demystified in a newer type of semantic science in which meanings are defined through a whole-part relationship.

Current science has, for many decades, attempted to create a theory of meaning through part-part relations. This attempt is logically inconsistent because it will produce many logically contradictory propositions. A logical system should not produce logical contradictions. A semantic science will overcome problems of logical inconsistency because the meaning of a part is defined through its relation to the whole. Since these meanings include conceptual and intentional relations, the part is expected to be *known* and *used* in accordance with its relation to the whole. If the part is known in a way that is different from its relation to the whole, that knowledge is incorrect. Similarly, if a part is used in a manner different from its relation to the whole, then the usage is wrong. Both incorrect knowledge and incorrect action are said to lead to bad *karma.*

The disparity between part-part relation and whole-part relation is a consequence of a discrepancy between *being* (i.e. what a thing is) and *knowing* (how we understand its nature) or *being* and *doing* (how we use that being). The *being*, in this case, is given by the whole-part relation while *knowing* and *acting* are based on our understanding of *part-part* relations. The consequences of our knowledge and action (also called *karma*), therefore, are essentially byproducts of the difference between reality and our perception of it, and reality and our actions based on a flawed perception. These gaps are considered epistemological and pragmatic problems in science. But these are also moral problems in Vedic philosophy.

This raises some interesting questions: If there is a gap between reality and its perception or between reality and its use, then there must indeed be some reality. How do we know this reality? This problem is answered based on the fact that reality is the part-whole relation. Therefore the true nature of a thing and its true use is how it relates to the whole. In Vedic philosophy, God is the ultimate whole. We have earlier discussed how this notion of whole defines the properties of space and time in the universe. We also saw how the whole appears as a part within the whole, as the first perfect instance of the idea embodied by the whole. The moral judgment about whether something is good or bad is therefore not a judgment of the effect our actions have on the other parts within the whole. The moral judgment is rather the effect our actions have on the whole. Accordingly, the moral law is God's law of nature.

In this view of morality, there isn't a moral law separate from God, and God does not obey that law. Rather, whatever God does or wants is moral because He is the whole. Morality is the relation between parts and wholes and actions of the part that accord with the whole are moral while actions that are in discord with the whole are immoral. The accord and discord are defined relative to the conceptual, intentional, and relational meanings in the parts (through their relation to the whole). These meanings define a role, purpose, and object relative to the whole. The object plays the role and fulfills a purpose, which sets the expectations for the part. The moral judgment is the difference between the expectation and reality. If a part fulfills the expectations, then there is no *karma*. If the part does less or more than what is expected from it, then *karma* is created.

Karma does not affect God because He is the whole. God is free of the consequences of His actions like any other living being who acts in relation to the whole. *Karma* affects other beings when their perception and action differ from those of God. Aligning our consciousness with the consciousness of God entails freedom from the consequences. This alignment is not a blind surrender to some fanatic ideology, but an understanding of reality and perfection in its use. The perfection in religion—i.e. the alignment between the consciousness in a soul and the consciousness in God—is also the perfection in scientific knowledge and the use of nature. This perfection is measured by freedom from the laws of material nature.

This brings us to the question that we began with. Do miracles violate scientific laws? As we saw, there are two kinds of laws—effects and consequences. God's actions don't violate the laws of effect. And He is not affected by the laws of consequence, in as much as other living beings can also act in a way that does not result in consequences. His actions therefore never violate scientific laws although they always transcend the laws of consequences.

Epilogue

At the beginning of this book, I spoke about a need for a radical conception of both science and religion. Religion, I said, had to provide a conception of God that related to the nature of space-time, matter, and causality in nature. Science too, I said, had to provide a conception of matter compatible with the existence of mind and consciousness. The current polemic between science and religion is based on a science that has no room for consciousness, and a religion that does not provide knowledge of God's relation to material nature.

Vedic philosophy is in a unique position to change the current notions of science and religion as it describes God's connection to matter and matter compatible with the existence of mind and consciousness. However, these notions about science and religion do not come without a substantial revision to the views widely held today. In science, we need to change the notions of matter, space-time, and causality from physical to semantic conceptions. This shift is indicated by the problems arising from attempts to incorporate meaning in matter. In religion, we need to shift our notions of God from someone Who stands apart from the creation to someone who creates the universe as His part. This shift is necessitated by the problem arising from attempts to explain the universe's origin.

Much of the conversation between science and religion today employs impersonalistic and voidistic stances towards religion because they seem to resonate with materialistic theories of nature, compared with a personal notion of a God as creator. The problem for impersonalism and voidism is to explain the arrival of diversity from oneness or nothingness. The personal approach to reality suffers from no such problem. In this approach, diversity is the consequence of a focus on different aspects of a person which separates the whole into parts. At some level, therefore, it is not false to suggest that there is a single whole and everything is a part of that whole. But it is incorrect to suggest that the whole's division into parts is temporary or illusory and only the undivided whole is real. The personalist approach allows for a single whole and many individuals, and these are not contradictory because the many individuals are parts of the same whole. In other words, the whole is eternally divided into parts, but that does not 'destroy' the whole's identity.

A revision to our notions about science and religion that steers clear of materialism in science and impersonalism and voidism in religion is a profound revolution in thinking. It will not only bring science and religion together but, more importantly, will prove religious ideas from within scientific theories. The latter possibility particularly excites me. As we saw through the course of this book, esoteric notions such as consciousness, supreme consciousness, mind, and morality all follow from a profound understanding of material nature. Given that the modern age is an age of reason and science, this is particularly interesting because it makes it possible to understand these difficult notions incrementally through problems in the study of material nature. In Vedic philosophy, there are many forms of God Who are connected to material nature to various extents. Their connection to nature makes a difference to the way nature is. This difference serves to illustrate the nature of God from the study of nature itself. A notion of God as the creator of nature thus changes the manner in which we can understand God from inside nature.

A rational understanding of God is not identical to religious experience. But it can very well separate true religious experience from illusions. Can we truly love a God that we don't understand? And how will we then separate this blind faith from ignorance? The answer to these problems is that the only way to fight blind faith and ignorance is to base our study of the nature of God on the same types of approaches that have currently been adopted in science. The problems in science, when suitably interpreted and solved, will not lead to materialism, impersonalism, or voidism. They will rather lead to a personalistic notion of God and a semantic understanding of nature. The former represents progress in religion while the latter represents progress in science. The combination of these two forms of knowledge and progress helps us understand the nature of our consciousness and its current predicament in the world.

God's existence, our consciousness and free will, and nature's lawfulness are therefore not contradictory ideas. There is a perspective that resolves the conflicts, addresses the problems, and paints a picture of nature, God, and ourselves that is more meaningful from the standpoints of both science and religion. The new viewpoint can provide a deeper understanding of matter, including the discovery of new properties and laws in nature. It can also facilitate a more rational foundation for religious and mystical experience.

Index

www.ingramcontent.com/pod-product-compliance
Lightning Source LLC
Chambersburg PA
CBHW020551030426
42337CB00013B/1050